RUNNING
WITH THE PACK

Also by Mark Rowlands

The Philosopher and the Wolf

RUNNING
WITH THE PACK

THOUGHTS FROM THE ROAD
ON MEANING AND MORTALITY

MARK ROWLANDS

PEGASUS BOOKS
NEW YORK LONDON

RUNNING WITH THE PACK

Pegasus Books LLC
80 Broad Street, 5th Floor
New York, NY 10004

Copyright © 2013 by Mark Rowlands
First Pegasus Books cloth edition November 2013

ISBN: 978-1-60598-477-3

10 9 8 7 8 6 5 4 3 2 1

Printed in the United States of America
Distributed by W. W. Norton & Company, Inc.

*This book is dedicated to the memory of
my father, Peter Rowlands.
The long run is over but your footsteps echo still.*

Contents

Foreword:
Running and Remembering

What is running? When a human being runs – in the recreational sense in which tens of millions of human beings do, in fact, run – what is the meaning or significance of this? One might think that the answer depends on the human being in question. Different people run for different reasons: some because they enjoy it, some because it makes them feel good, look good, because it keeps them healthy, happy, even alive. Some run for company, others to relieve the stress of everyday life. Some like to push themselves, test their limits; others like to compare their limits with the limits of others. It seems obvious that the significance of running varies from one person to another, because this significance simply amounts to the reasons a person has for running.

Nevertheless, it is currently popular to think that running has a meaning or significance not simply for individual human beings but for humans as a whole. This significance, many think, is grounded in the role running played in our evolutionary past and so in making us – all of us – what we are today. Some think, and they may be right, that we are simians that were born to run – designed by millions of years of random mutation and natural selection to be running apes.

We ran so that we could hunt, so that we could eat animals and not just plants. And, as Harvard anthropologist Richard Wrangham and others have argued, the resulting increase in protein in our diet played at least some role in the significant expansions our brains underwent during this time. It may not have been the driving force behind this 'encephalization', but without this increase in protein it could not have happened. Running, in other words, removed an important constraint on our development as a species. Others have postulated an even closer connection between our ancestral running and our impressive contemporary cognitive abilities. Our ancestors' hunting strategy was based not on speed but endurance – on the ability to keep track of a single animal, even if it was a member of a large herd, and track it mile after mile, keep up the pressure on it, to force it to keep running until it eventually died of overheating. Bernd Heinrich, a biologist at the University of Vermont, has argued that this necessity of focusing on one animal to the exclusion of all others, keeping that attention focused as the animal disappears towards the horizon, and maintaining it during the hours or even days to come, was the foundation of all our cognitive powers.

I think these stories, like many of the stories we tell about ourselves, are important not so much because of what they say but what they show. In saying this, I do not mean to suggest that the stories are necessarily false. On the contrary, I think there are important elements of truth in them. But an element of truth mistaken for a whole truth is sometimes more damaging than a lie. These evolutionary explanations of the significance of running attempt to account for this significance in terms of the usefulness that running has for the species *Homo sapiens*. There is nothing wrong with this: that is the way evolutionary explanations do and must work.

But implicit in this – and this is what the stories show – is the assignation to running of value of a certain sort. Running is valuable because of what it does. Running is valuable because of other things it has brought us.

The assignation of this sort of value is reiterated at the level of the individual when we explain the significance of running in terms of the reasons people have for running. Individual people run, it is assumed, because it is useful for them to do so, in one way or another. Philosophers often refer to this value that derives from usefulness as 'instrumental' value. Something has instrumental value when it has value as an instrument – as a means to an end. Money has instrumental value: its value lies in the value of the things it can buy you. Medicine has instrumental value: its value lies in the value of the health to which it can restore you. When something has merely instrumental value, it does not have value in itself – its value always lies elsewhere, in something else. It is this other thing that is the real locus of value.

Running does have instrumental value. But the error implicit in both accounts of running, individual and evolutionary – an error that is perhaps great enough to be considered a monstrous historical lie – is to suppose that this is the only value running has. It is not – it is not even the primary value running has.

We live, in certain respects, in a monstrous age. This instrumentalist way of thinking about running is a reflection of the narrowly utilitarian era in which we have grown up: a time where everything must have a use – must be 'good for something'. In his seminal essay, 'The Question Concerning Technology', Martin Heidegger, perhaps the most important philosopher of the twentieth century, argued that implicit in the modern age is what he called a *Gestell* – an 'enframing'. That is, the modern age embodies a way of seeing or understanding the world around us and, as such, precludes other ways of seeing this world. The modern age is by no means unique in this regard: all the ages of humans have their defining *Gestell*. The characteristic of the modern age is a *Gestell* of a singularly instrumental or utilitarian form. In the *Gestell* of the modern world, everything is reduced to a resource of some or other sort. We encounter and understand things only in terms of their use – broadly speaking, in terms of what they might do for us, whether for good or ill – and we fail to even understand that there might be anything else of value to them. Even the world of nature is now described as a collection of natural resources. Heidegger, with his characteristic penchant for ungrammaticality, described this instrumentalizing tendency of modern thought as a 'darkened of the world'. Reality itself is understood in narrowly technological terms.

Perhaps it is too strong to say that we have become constitutionally unable to think of value in any other terms than as a function of use. But we do find it difficult. Certainly, that is the way the activity of running is typically justified, both to oneself and others. One runs, so one says, to stay healthy, to stay thin, to relax, to stay alive. The implicit assumption in these answers is that if running is a legitimate way of spending one's time, then it must be 'good for something': that is, it must be useful in some way. That running may have a value that is independent of what it can do for us – that it might have a value that cannot be understood in instrumental terms – is an idea we find difficult to even understand. I say this from experience. I had to overcome many years of confusion, decades in fact, before I understood this.

I will spend much time in this book describing the

experience of running – conducting, as philosophers some-times put it, a 'phenomenological' investigation. I do not do this just for the sake of it, or because I enjoy it – in fact I find it a difficult, exacting, often wearying thing to do. Rather, I describe the experience of running because, I shall argue, it is the experience of a kind of value that is quite different – value that is not instrumental, not a function of usefulness. And in this value one can discern, at least in broad outline, something that is important in life. In this book, I shall defend a claim that many, I think most, will find strange. It is true that running has multifarious forms of instrumental value. However, at its purest and its best, running has an entirely different sort of value. This is sometimes known as 'intrinsic' or 'inherent' value. To say that something has intrinsic value is to say that it is valuable for what it is in itself, and not because of anything else it might allow one to get or possess. Running, I shall argue, is intrinsically valu-able. And so when one runs, and does this for the right reason, one is in contact with intrinsic value in life.

This has a significance that is far broader then merely understanding the essence of running – what running really is. Living amidst the darkened of the world, our lives are marred by the inability to recognize intrinsic value when we encounter it. Our lives are lived doing one thing for the sake of something else, which is in turn done for the sake of another something else. Three score years and ten, or twenty, of an endless for-the-sake-of-which: decades of chasing what is valuable but only rarely catching it. To be in contact with something that is important for its own sake, and not merely for the sake of something else, would be to end this chase, at least for a while. For a time at least, one does not chase value, one is immersed in it.

People sometimes ask – this is after all what philosophers are supposed to do, though few of us these days do it – what is the meaning of this life? The question is unfortunately constructed in at least two respects. First, the word 'meaning' has suggested to some people that the answer we are looking for is a mystical one, of the sort that might be supplied by a guru. Secondly, the use of the definite article suggests that the question permits only one answer – a sort of existential magic bullet that will tell us unequivocally what life is all about. But, in reality, the question is more familiar and less ambitious: a question that almost everyone will ask himself or herself at some time or other. What is important in life? Alternatively: what is valuable in life? Or: what should I cherish in life? Or, if we assume that the way I live will reflect the things I value: how should I live? Mystical answers to these questions are of little use: an answer would be useful to the extent it can be understood, and to the extent it can be understood it is not mystical. Moreover, there is no reason to suppose these questions admit of only one answer.

Running, I shall argue, is a way of understanding what is important or valuable in life. It is a way of putting oneself in contact with intrinsic value as it shows itself, or makes itself known, in a human life. Running is by no means the only way of doing this. But it is one way: and as such it is a way of answering the question of the meaning of life, in the only reasonable sense this question can have – however mundane and unambitious that may be. The answer to this question is, at least for me, always tenuous and shifting. It is something I understand only in moments, and then it is gone. But these may be the most important moments of my life. Fundamentally, I shall try to convince you that there is a type of knowledge embodied in running. When I run, I know what is important in life – although for many years I did not know that I knew this. This is not so much knowledge newly acquired as knowledge reclaimed. When I was a boy, I also knew what was important in life. I suspect we all did, although we did not know that we knew it. But this is something I forgot when I began the great game of growing up and becoming someone. Indeed, it is something I had to forget in order to play this game at all. It is one of life's great ironies that those least in need of understanding its meaning are those who most naturally and effortlessly understand it. On the long run, I can hear the whispers of a childhood I can never reclaim, and of a home to which I can never return. In these whispers, in the rumours and mutterings of the long run, there are moments when I understand again what it was I once knew.

Thoughts sit on a printed page, but they echo through a life – the echoes of a bell that tolls slowly in the distance. But rather than simply replicating the peal that produced it, the echo is always subtly transformed: always transformed because life is always moving. This is the Doppler shift of thought as it occurs in a life; the mutation of thought that is lived and not merely thought. A book about running, I slowly came to understand, must have the structure of running; if not, the thoughts that make it up just will not fit and so will not make sense. Running is undifferentiated activity. Every movement – every stride of the long run, every swing of the arms – flows into the next. The thoughts that make up this book are like that. They flow into each other, never constant, never stable, always changing, shifting as the run goes on.

The separation into chapters is, in some respects, nominal. The chapters are organized around runs, discrete episodes in my life and the life of the pack that ran with me, but the thoughts that animate these runs flow into each other. From the perspective of thought, if not life, each chapter begins where the last chapter ends – even though the runs they describe might be separated by many years. Ideas that I thought I had left in the dust miles back, years back, insist on reappearing in new and subtly mutated forms. Logic: that is still there, but not so much as the legs and arms that drive the run as the signposts that direct it. The book does not unfold as a logical argument should, with premises that neatly, efficiently and decisively yield conclusions. Rather, this book is the record of someone struggling to run – as on many of my runs, often slowly and painfully – in the general direction of a conclusion. I will get there in the end. But on this run, there are many dead ends, no through roads and blind alleys. Sometimes, even the roads that actually go somewhere had to be run and rerun over and over again before I understood where they led. I apologize if there may sometimes appear to be repetition. In reality, the routes are always subtly changing, both in landscape and destination, and that is one of the most important things about them. In the end, the run always takes us home, back to where we started. But sometimes, if we run long enough, that home will have become transformed. The end of this book is also its beginning. But if the book has worked, that beginning will have been decisively changed.

I sometimes think that running may be a place where I channel my history. Running is a place where I really do stand on the shoulders of giants – or, more appositely, run in the conceptual slipstream of thinkers older and better than I – a place where things that I have read and seemingly forgotten, things that have become buried long, long years in the trivialities of life and the life of the trivial, once again have their moment on the conscious stage, to strut and pout and remonstrate: why did you forget me? This stage they enter and exit, changing nothing or changing everything, and I have little say in any of it. Running is a place where I remember. Most importantly, it is a place where I remember not the thoughts of others, but something that I once knew, a lifetime ago, but was forced to forget in the process of growing up and becoming someone. I knew this although I did not know that I knew it; and in this I was just like everyone else. Running is a place for remembering. It is in this place that we find the meaning of running.

RUNNING
WITH THE PACK

1

The Starting Line
2011

This could go one of several ways, all of them ugly. Daybreak
is still around an hour away. What remains of the night sees
me standing in corral G, slap, bang in the middle of around
20,000 people, my immediate vicinity seemingly populated
exclusively by pumped-up septuagenarians. They surround
me – these ancient pots and pans bubbling over with excited
anticipation, detailing the times and split times they're
expecting to run. I am feeling a little less sanguine. Emil
Zatopek, the great Czech distance runner of the 1950s, once
said: 'If you want to run, run a mile. But if you want to experience another life, run a marathon.' I wouldn't know, I've
never run a marathon before. But it does strike me that my
training for the marathon did tend to follow the general contours of life: a promising, but essentially misleading, start –
and then it all went downhill. There are around 52,000 steps
between here and the finish line, and I have no idea if I'm
going to be able to complete more than a hundred of them.

It had all been going so well. In fact, I clearly remember boring my wife with interminable commentaries on how I had utterly nailed the preparations for my first marathon. It's not that difficult, really. Most people can run a marathon if they put their mind to it. But, there again, most people are far too sensible to want to put their mind to it. If you are already running around twenty miles a week – say four runs of five miles each – then you are only about four months away from being able to run your first marathon. In fact, I wasn't even running that much when I started my preparation. The cornerstone of this preparation is what is known as the 'long run'. This will typically be done on a weekend. The week is then reserved for shorter, faster runs. I started with three short runs of four miles during the week. The short runs always stay relatively short – when my training was in full swing, I was running six miles, eight miles and six miles during the week.

The long run is really the key to training for a marathon. On the long run, you keep your pace down to something that allows you to hold a conversation, or would allow you to do this if there were anyone else there. I run only with my dog, Hugo, who is not the best conversationalist. For me, that pace was just a little over five miles an hour. Then, holding this pace more or less constant, you gradually build up the distance, week by week, mile by mile. The first, and rather inglorious, long run of my training regime was a pathetic six miles. In my defence, this was September in Miami: the temperature was in the mid-nineties and the humidity made it seem ten degrees hotter than that. People who have never run before in serious heat and humidity are shocked at just how much more difficult it is. I know I was. Your heart and lungs have to work so much harder just to keep you cool in those conditions. Sometimes, I would find myself sucking in air, like I had just come off the back of a series of sprints. But I slowly built up the distance – an extra mile per week, give or take. That, I suppose, was not as easy as it sounds. Every week, the last extra mile was a killer. I ran it if I could, I walked it if I had to. The key was simply to stay on my feet and keep moving forward. By early December 2010, I had my long run up to twenty miles – and for a marathon virgin like me, the long run never really goes above twenty miles. I was set.

There were still two months to go until the race, and so I did what I usually do in these situations: I broke my own cardinal rule. When I first decided to run this race, I told myself in no uncertain terms that I was not going to even think about times. This was my first marathon, and my goal was simply to negotiate the 26.2 miles without dying. Whatever you do, Mark, I told myself, just focus on that. You're not young any more – less than two years to the big five-o in fact. Your goal is simply to finish. Don't get caught up in anything else. But then December arrived, I was running twenty miles without too much difficulty and I started thinking. I could fit in another five or six of these long runs before race day, even allowing for the tapering-down in the final few weeks of training. I could really work on getting the times down. I could not only run this race, I could run a respectable time. Maybe not four hours, but 4.30 is definitely on; even 4.15 is not beyond the bounds of possibility. And so, a recurring theme of many of the best tragedies, it was my unseemly ambition that brought me down. My body threw in the towel when I started asking it to do this extra distance in less time.

When it happens, a grade-two tear of the calf muscle feels like someone has whacked you across the back of the leg with a stick. But I knew that already. Grade-two calf tears and I go back a long way – back to the mid-1990s, I seem to remember. The typical rehab for this sort of calf tear, for someone of my age, is six weeks plus. If the patient turns out not to be patient at all – and I am a very impatient patient – then that period extends accordingly. I treated this particular tear with more than usual deference, at least initially. I did my rehab, got the scar tissue broken down and did all the exercises my PT told me to do. Then, just as I started getting better, I lost all patience, tried to run, my calf broke down again after a few hundred yards and I was back to square one. This happened several times. So eventually I just did nothing: complete rest. The tear occurred on 4 December 2010. It is now 30 January 2011. I am standing at the starting line of the Miami Marathon – and, more significantly for me, my first marathon – and I haven't been able to run for the two months leading up to it.

I am therefore, as they say, a little 'undercooked' – and that's probably putting it mildly. Until Friday lunchtime, if you had asked me whether I was going to run, I would have told you 'no' – or some more emphatic variation on that theme. And I think I would have almost been sincere. This was the official position that I used not only in my dealings with others but also, more importantly, with the rational part of my mind. But there was a small, sneaky, irrational but enormously influential part of me that always knew that I was going to find myself standing at the starting line of this race. So I wasn't entirely surprised to find myself driving over to the Miami Beach Convention Center on Friday afternoon to pick up my race packet. I still had to deal with the rational part of me, of course. Just keeping our options open, I told it. Indeed, my rational self replied, is that why you also purchased a calf sleeve, and interrogated just about every runner you met at the Center about how to approach running a marathon when in a seriously under-trained state? That's the rational part of me – he can occasionally be a little snide. But despite the abundance of countervailing evidence, I think I was still spouting the 'just keeping my options open' line when I crawled onto the train at 4 a.m. this morning. But now, it seems, the time for options is over. Perhaps I should have listened a little more to the rational part of me. This was all very preventable.

The most likely scenario, given the events of recent weeks, is that my calf immediately breaks down again and I don't even make it as far as the MacArthur Causeway. I suppose that would be a little humiliating – my abject failure on display to the thousands who run past me. But suppose it doesn't happen like that: suppose my calf pulls itself together. Then the question is: how long will it be before I am wishing that it had gone? I'm not entirely sure what sort of shape I'm going to be in, but I suspect it's not going to be good. Just how far am I going to be able to go? I could always call it a day at the half-marathon mark. But will I even get that far? Just how painful is this going to be?

Then there is the question of time. Suppose I do make it around the course. Just how long is that going to take me? This has nothing to do with pride. Well, if I am being honest, I suppose it may have something to do with it but, vanity aside, the one thing you absolutely, positively don't want to do in the Miami Marathon is take your own sweet time about it. There is, as in most city marathons, a graduated reopening of the roads. You want to stay ahead of these reopenings if you can. After six hours, all the roads are open again. Having to finish the race weaving my way in and out of traffic would not only be somewhat mortifying – it would be positively dangerous.

I've been in many countries where the drivers are clearly insane. Greece and France spring to mind. But in those countries the vehicular psychosis is more or less predictable. After you've been there a while, you can more or less predict which senseless gambit is going to occur in what situation. After a while, it all seems wearyingly quotidian. But in Miami, nothing that has to do with the roads is predictable. There is no public transport in Miami worth speaking of. The city's elevated monorail has, as the writer Dave Barry once put it, about as much significance in the life of the average Miamian as a shooting star occasionally glimpsed out of the corner of one's eye. Everyone drives. And so the demographic runs from boy racers to boozed-up businessmen to heavily medicated centenarians, even the occasional heavily-medicated-boozed-up-centenarian-boy-racer. No one really has a clue what's going to happen at any given junction. And since a significant percentage of them are armed – the medicated centenarians, especially, seem to like to drive a little 'heavy' – remonstration is a dangerous game to play.

On YouTube yesterday, while I was 'researching' my run, I found a video record of last year's race entitled, unfortunately not inaccurately: 'Scumbag Miami drivers honk marathon runners.' The humiliation of immediate calf breakdown, a protracted and painful run, or mortality by vehicular means: disappointment, pain or death – Zatopek may have had a point. This is certainly going to be ugly. I feel a strange tingling, something I haven't felt for quite some time. Is it fear? Perhaps that is a little aggrandizing. Let's just say I'm nervous. And it is not entirely unpleasant.

Why am I doing this? It's not an easy question to answer, and to avoid trying to do so, when people ask me this, I am more than happy to resort to platitudes. I could say, 'Because I enjoy it.' In some sense of the word, I enjoyed the training – while it lasted – and I am enjoying the trepidation of these pre-race minutes. I am enjoying the feeling that I may have bitten off more than I can chew; I am enjoying the uncertainty – the not knowing what is going to happen next. In some sense of 'enjoy', I might even enjoy what is going to happen next. So there would be a modicum of truth in this 'enjoyment' answer. But it's not a particularly illuminating modicum – it is not the sort of truth that advances understanding, but merely invites the further question: why do I enjoy these things? I could add: I'll soon be fifty, and if I don't do it now, I'll probably never do it. And it would be a shame to have lived a whole life and never run a marathon. I am sure that's part of the reason; but it is still just a stock answer, and vulnerable to the same sort of objection as the original response. After all, why do I think it would be a shame to have lived a whole life and never run a marathon? The real reasons, I suspect, are more difficult to identify, let alone explain. But it is an interesting sociological fact that (a) many people seem to have opinions on what my reasons are, and (b) the content of these opinions depends on where – specifically which side of the Atlantic – those people live.

There is, I think, a distinctively American way of thinking about running and, by extension, about what I am doing today. Books written by Americans about running almost always revolve around certain recognizable themes. In saying this, I don't mean in any way to disparage them. I've read quite a few of these books – from Dean Karnazes's inspiring *Ultramarathon Man*, to Christopher McDougall's astonishing *Born to Run*, to Bernd Heinrich's (whom I shall regard as an honorary American since he has lived in the US most of his life) engaging *Why We Run*, and many more. But even in these thoroughly admirable books, the shared themes are evident, and this is what makes these books quintessentially American.

One theme is an unflinching pioneer optimism. You can do great things. Everyone has this capacity. Every day, you can be better than you were yesterday; and there is nothing that exceeds your grasp if you put your mind to it. This sort of optimism is, of course, a semi-ubiquitous mantra of American life. I love this belief, and I find its profession, by large swathes of the American population, touching and sincere. The only problem is that I'm pretty sure it's not true. Most things lie outside the grasp of most people. And the one unbreakable truth of life is that we get worse. Maybe you could do great things. Maybe you still can. Maybe you successfully completed an unspeakably brutal ultramarathon yesterday – *Badwater*, *Leadville*, the *Marathon des Sables* or something like that. I don't know. But I do know that you will get worse. If you can do great things, then the time is coming when you won't be able to do them any more.

Another theme is the emphasis on faith. Faith is what gets you through the inevitable dark times you will face on the run. Faith is, it goes without saying, a cornerstone of American life. Faith makes us strong; we are at our best when we have faith. But I – a European of shadowed soul, skulking in the middle of the starting pack – suspect that, on the contrary, we are at our best when we have lost our faith. In fact, this was, arguably, the principal message of my earlier book, *The Philosopher and the Wolf.* The loss of faith is, precisely, an opportunity to grow stronger. In the end, I believe the only attitude we can bring to bear on life that is worth anything at all is defiance. Not that it makes any difference in the end, of course: it is going to end badly for us, whatever we do – if not, our defiance would of course be singularly misplaced. Compared to the sprightly sales figures in Europe and other parts of the world, sales of the US edition of *The Philosopher and the Wolf* were, I think it is fair to say, 'sluggish' – a term which will also almost certainly be applicable to any progress I make in today's race. I have absolutely no faith that I will finish this race or even get very far in it – and, for me, this is part of the attraction. What's the point in trying something if you know or strongly suspect – whether it is through faith or any other means – you will succeed? In fact, I suspect it is precisely my suspicion that I haven't a hope of finishing that is one of the primary attractions for me today.

Finally, American running books will emphasize the positive value of work. Two different strands of this idea can be distinguished. Some seem to think that work is inherently ennobling. Others tie the value of work to the dreams it allows you to grasp (see the first 'optimism' strand). But my murky European spirit tells me that work is not inherently ennobling at all: to work when you do not have to is stupid rather than ennobling. And there is no evidence of any reliable connection between hard work and realization of dreams. Nothing good comes of work, I tell myself. At its best, and its most valuable, running is play not work. This is one of the things I actually learned through running.

Optimism, faith and work: I want nothing of these things. Apparently, I am a faithless pessimist who thinks that hard work is worthless. It is a little surprising they gave me a Green Card.

I am running this marathon because I have lost my faith. Perhaps that is a step in the direction of the truth? Imagine a toothless crocodile with Alzheimer's looking for a hat that is already on his head. This was my brother's classic 1993 'Fossil of the Week' birthday card to my father; perhaps the apotheosis of a family tradition of sending each other insulting, and preferably cruel, birthday cards. We put a lot of time, effort and ingenuity into finding exactly the right one. It's the thought that counts.

Perhaps my most telling contribution to this tradition was the 2007 triumph on the occasion of my brother's fortieth birthday. That card comprised a group of boy scouts on a camping trip. A boy is telling a scary story illuminated, as tradition dictates, by a torch pressed under his chin. The faces of his audience express terror and disbelief. This is the snippet of the story to which we are privy: 'And then hair starts growing out of your nose and ears!' The card's message: *some horror stories are true.*

A few days before my forty-eighth birthday, and a few months before finding myself at this starting line of a marathon, I received a worthy riposte. Two bats are hanging upside down (that is the card's salient visual fact). One says to the other:

'You know what frightens me most about old age?'

'No. What?'

'Incontinence.'

The function of religion is to make us feel better, by peddling a lie. The function of philosophy, and a carefully chosen birthday card, is to make us feel worse, by telling the truth. And the truth is of course: we get worse.

Around the time this card was winging its way to me over the Atlantic, I found myself asking my GP a question: 'What do you mean, *gout*?'

About a week before, I had woken in the middle of the night

and noticed that the big toe on my left foot had stiffened up. The next morning, walking was painful. And then it just got more and more painful. In a few days time, my entire foot had swollen up and was far too painful for me to wear shoes. I hobbled barefoot into the doctor's office to see what was up. If my question was a simple one, its answer was deceptively revealing; not so much in what it said, but in what it showed.

'Well, it does look like gout. We can't be sure without a blood test to find out your uric acid levels.'

'I don't have gout. Old, overweight people get gout.'

'Well, it is true that obesity and hypertension raise your risk of gout, but they're not prerequisites.'

'But gout! That's Henry VIII – a diet of goose legs and gallons of wine, that sort of thing. I'm a vegetarian you know.'

'Well, yes, a diet that is high in purines, like meat and fish, increases the risk of gout. It's interesting that you're a vegetarian. Do you drink much?'

'Drink much, me? Well … you know, a little dry sherry at Christmas time. Look I'm a writer; I think I'm contractually obligated to drink. I'll be honest. In my formative years, yes, I could put it away; but not any more, not since the boys came along. They show no mercy, you know. If I wake up a little fuzzy-headed, they can smell weakness, like sharks smelling blood. It's going to be a long, long day for me. It's just not worth it. I might have a glass or two of wine with dinner, after the boys have gone to bed, but that's it. Occasionally three, occasionally one: never more than three, though.'

'Ah, aversion therapy: interesting. Would this be every night?'

'Well … you know, most nights. Unless I'm going out or something – then I have to drive, so I don't drink, of course. But I don't go out much.'

'Alcohol consumption is shown to be implicated in gout attacks nearly half the time.'

'So I need to give up?'

'No, nothing drastic like that. But you might want to take a night or two off, every now and then. Give your kidneys a break.'

'Okay, that certainly doesn't sound unreasonable, doctor. But, you really think it is gout?'

'Well, it might be something else. Have you ever damaged this toe, broken it, dislocated it?'

'Actually, now you mention it, I seem to remember dislocating it years ago, back in my karate days.'

'Oh, that's unfortunate. If there's joint damage, there's a possibility of it being osteo-arthritis. You wouldn't want that. It's nasty. Gout is much easier to manage. The other thing it might be is a stress fracture. You said you run?'

'Yes, but not so much lately. There were times when I would run forty miles a week, a long run of twenty miles, stuff like that. But those days are gone – well, at least in Miami. I hate running here: too hot, too humid, too flat, and you're under permanent assault from mosquitoes. But I do have a young dog that needs a lot of exercise. So we do a few miles most days. Nothing drastic, though. I don't run marathons or anything like that.'

'I suppose there's an outside chance that it's a stress fracture, which would be very unfortunate – difficult to get rid of. But I really don't think so. It's usually the twenty-somethings that come in here with stress fractures. And it does look like gout. So, what I'm going to do is give you a cortisone shot in the joint. That'll kill it dead.

'Will it hurt?'

He smiles: 'It'll hurt like hell.'

And it did. But it certainly did the trick. Cortisone is good shit.

So gout, Wikipedia tells me, is the result of a build-up of uric acid crystals in the joints. Uric acid comes from urea, a by-product of protein breakdown. If your kidneys are not doing their job properly, then urea will not be eliminated from the blood quickly enough and will form into crystals of uric acid. These collect in the joints – the joint at the base of the big toe is typical – and will be treated as foreign bodies by the immune system. The resulting melee causes a gouty attack.

But that is not important. The truly revealing part of this little chapter in the book of my general demise is the background of assumptions it reveals. I've reached that point in life where gout is the best-case scenario; gout is what I should be hoping for. And so, in my primary care physician's office, the monstrous nature of life was illuminated for me once again. As if I needed it. One day you are running twenty miles for fun. The next, you are keeping your fingers crossed for gout.

I entered myself in the 2011 ING Miami Marathon the next day, and embarked on a strict training regime – part of a new policy of showing my failing body who was boss. A few months later, around the time my calf was making its protestations known, I received the results of the blood work. My uric acid levels were normal. My painful toe was almost certainly not gout. In fact, it seems a far more likely cause was the running I had been doing to keep Hugo happy. So I had apparently upped my running to address a problem that was caused by running. My entry into the world of marathon running was, in this sense, a deeply ironic one.

But the toe, that is only a symptom – a gentle scratching of the surface of a more global decline. Some horror stories are true. What young person would not be disgusted by their older self? It was a promising start, a few halcyon years of thrusting, burgeoning vitality. But they didn't last long. Then it was all downhill, physically and intellectually. There is life and there is death. That's the way people usually think of it. Death is the end of life, and so is not a part of life. Death is not an event in my life, as Wittgenstein once said. I suspect the truth is a little more complex.

First, instead of thinking of life as one thing and death as another, I tend to think more in terms of a gradual process of disappearing. Life, fundamentally, is a process of erasure. After a promising, but as it turns out essentially disingenuous, first couple of decades or so, I slowly become less and less of what I was. Death is an admittedly significant point in this process – a late and irreversible stage of my disappearance. But erasure doesn't stop there. Not content with my destruction, the process rumbles on until every trace I might have left, any indication that I was once here, is also obliterated. So, instead of thinking in crude dichotomous terms – life–death – I apparently like to think in crude trichotomous terms instead: decline + death + deletion = disappearance.

Conversely, it would be an error to think of death as an event safely cordoned off in the future. Death is impatient and insists on putting in little appearances before the curtain goes down; little cameos that gradually increase in their frequency and transparency. As the outstanding, and perhaps for that reason largely forgotten, Hungarian phenomenologist Aurel Kolnai pointed out: the basis of all disgust is death in life. Our decline is really death creeping up on us in various ways, sneaking us various little previews of what lies in store. My apparently gouty toe is a swollen, putrid corpse appendage. The hard body of my twenties slowly becomes

14

soft and slack, like an orange that has sat in the bowl a few days longer than it should. The hairs that sprout from various parts of me, parts from which, I would have thought, they have no business sprouting, these are opportunistic colonies of mould that have made this overripe orange their home. In these ways and others, my death likes to exhibit itself long before the end of the show.

Perhaps these little cameos should produce in me nothing more than a wry smile. Death does have a sense of humour, I might tell myself. Julian Barnes tells a story of a former soldier, worn down by life, who asked Julius Caesar, his former general, for permission to end his life. Caesar replied: what makes you think that what you have now is life? Caesar also had a sense of humour, just not a good one. No doubt he was being a little harsh, a little premature. But we are all now aware of the idea of a person disappearing before the end of their biological life. This is a recurring horror of mine. I've seen the closing years of enough lives to understand the levels of fear and confusion embodied in them. To approach death is gradually, progressively, to become un-homed. 'I just want to go home now,' my dying grandmother once said to me from her nursing home. And so I imagine myself in years to come telling some person I do not know that I just want to go home now. But in this future there is no home. Soon, I'll not even remember what a home is.

So I am running this marathon, perhaps, because some horror stories are true. There is a part of me that likes this explanation. There is a comforting familiarity – even nostalgia – that accompanies it. Circumstances have seen me live much of my adult life outside Britain, but I'm still enough of a Brit to recognize the age-old tradition of taking an activity that someone does and finding ways to denigrate it – ideally by casting aspersions on the motives or character of the person doing it. I appreciate this tradition for the cultural art form that it is – even when I am the person whose motives or character are thus aspersed. Now I know why I'm running this marathon. *It's a midlife crisis, mate.*

And yet I am far from alone in my new avocation. I'm part of a rapidly growing cultural phenomenon – the forty-something who has become obsessed with testing the limits of his or her endurance. In this respect, my efforts are embarrassingly feeble. Forget marathons: ultra running events – foot races of fifty miles, a hundred miles or more – are springing up everywhere. Possibly the hardest is *Badwater*. This is a 135-mile foot race that incorporates a significant chunk of California: beginning in Death Valley, at 282 feet below sea level, and finishing 8642 feet higher, at Whitney Portal – the trailhead of Mount Whitney, the highest peak in the state. In the early parts of the run, temperatures can reach 130°F. If you take bread into the open air at that temperature, it begins to toast. The tarmac is so hot your shoes will start to melt, and so you have to run on the white line at the side of the road – cooler because it reflects heat. Then there is the *Marathon des Sables*, a six-day 151-mile foot race across the Sahara Desert. Runners have to carry anti-venom syringes with them, because of the numerous snakes that litter the route. Or, if you are tired of the heat, there's the *Hardrock* – 100 miles run at altitudes of over 14,000 feet in the Colorado Rockies – a slow and difficult race that involves scrambling up and down improbably steep hills, and where the principal medical problems include high-altitude cerebral oedema. Many of the finishers take over forty-eight hours to complete this race, which means – given that the start is just before dawn – that they will see the sun rise three times during their time spent running. Then there is *Leadville* – another Colorado Rockies 14,000-feet, 100-mile offering, centred on the USA's highest city – where the completion rate is lower than the *Hardrock*.

I must admit: I have been bitten by the bug. Those races are monsters that may always be beyond me. But if I can get my calf right, I do have my beady little eye on some softer fifty-milers for later in the year. Are we endurance freaks all suffering from our own midlife crises? Did it use to be – as caricature would suggest, at least for men – inappropriately young women and sports cars, whereas now it's the *Badwater* or *Marathon des Sables*?

I suppose, if this interpretation is correct, we would have to expand the idea of a midlife crisis, make it more inclusive and gender-neutral. This 'crisis' is far from an exclusively male thing. As many women as men have been bitten by the endurance bug. And in their resulting avocation, they can compete with men on a more or less equal footing. Apparently, no woman is going to give Usain Bolt a run for his money. But the longer the distance of the race, the more the gap between men and women narrows. Ann Trason wins 100-mile ultras outright, at least she used to. It is true, I expect, that women have midlife crises too. But the main problem is supposing that the label 'midlife crisis' explains anything at all.

Labelling something is often done to stop thinking about it, just when the hard thinking should be starting. We need to dig deeper. What is a midlife crisis? What is its essence? In particular, does the *Hardrock* or *Marathon des Sables* type of midlife crisis have anything in common with the classic but clichéd younger-woman/fast-car midlife crisis? Perhaps there is something that the two alleged crises have in common.

But until I can identify precisely what that is, the label 'midlife crisis' means nothing.

There is a way of thinking about a midlife crisis that ties it closely to the idea of achievement. A midlife crisis is the result of the realization that your abilities are on the wane, and consequently that your reach is henceforth condemned to exceed your grasp by an ever-increasing, and perhaps ultimately embarrassing, margin. The younger-woman/fast-car response is an attempt to reassert youth's authority of grasp over reach. Is this what it is all about?

Of course, I can only speak for myself. But the reassertion of grasp over reach hypothesis – the idea that running is all about achievement – just doesn't convince me. I think one of the things I quickly learned from running was the futility of achievement. Most of the running I have done in my life has not been about achievement anyway – not as far as I can see. It was just something I did, for a variety of reasons. Entering this race, I suppose, does introduce an element of achievement into the mix. But, even then, the achievement in question is of a peculiarly self-undermining variety. When I started training for this marathon, six miles in the Miami late-summer heat would nearly kill me. Slowly I built up the distance. I could barely sleep the nights before my long runs, I was so eager to get out on the road to see if I could do the extra distance. But as soon as I did, the immediate feeling of satisfaction was quickly replaced by restlessness. Twelve miles, okay – but next week I'll do thirteen. Learning to run distance is all about setting reasonable weekly goals – goals you can achieve if you put in the work – and then achieving them. This seems to be hard work followed by achievement: one strand of the American Dream. But, for me at least, I

18

don't know how it is with others, this is a very special sort of work-achievement cycle. It is a work-achievement cycle that reveals the futility of all work-achievement cycles. Running distance is goal-based achievement that reveals the bankruptcy of goal-based achievement.

Imagine you are a little kid outside a sweet shop, penniless, staring in at all the sweets you can't buy. God appears next to you and says:

'You know, kid, one day you'll be able to buy everything in this shop.'

'Really, God?'

'Yep, and you know what? When you can, you won't want to anymore. That's life, kid!'

Any worthwhile achievement, I suspect, changes you in a way that makes what you achieve no longer important to you. If by some miracle I actually finish this marathon, I'll have a celebratory late brunch – aka a bucketful of Mojitos – on South Beach. But I guarantee you that by dinner time my initial surge of satisfaction will be replaced by restlessness. The first thing I think will be this: well, after all, I did it, and on the back of a seriously curtailed training regime as well – I mean, how difficult can it be? Then, I'll start thinking about the Keys 100 – an ultramarathon (with 50- or 100-mile options, take your pick) from Key Largo to Key West that's happening in May. Then, I'll start thinking about some altogether more challenging things that are in the pipeline for late 2011 and 2012. But the goal of this is not to achieve things. To think that it is would be to misunderstand everything. I don't want a stack of race completion certificates I can put on my living-room wall or medals or belt buckles that tell people: I've run this, I've run that. The sense of satisfaction that goes with knowing I have finished a race? I don't even want that. Achievement, for me at least, is a process of making the things I achieve not matter any more. I run not to achieve anything – not in this sense of acquiring something – but to be changed by the process of achieving. Of course, I have to achieve things in order to be changed by a process of achieving things. But achieving things is just a means to an end. I run because I want to be changed. The question is of course: how?

Another way of thinking about the midlife crisis is as an attempt to reclaim the freedom of youth. This I think is partly right, but also wrong in at least one crucial respect. Running distance is about freedom – I'm convinced of that – but it's not the same sort as the freedom of youth. Both the traditional midlife crisis and the endurance-based alternative are, in their own ways, about freedom. But where they differ – and they do differ crucially – is that they have a very different conception of what freedom is.

In the high-velocity sports of my youth – rugby, cricket, boxing and tennis – the distinction between body and mind was at its most attenuated. In those endeavours, where missiles or hands or entire human bodies were hurtling towards me intent on mischief, there was no distinction between mind and body. In those days, in those sports, I was my lived body. Sometimes I wouldn't even know I was doing something until after I had done it. I remember the best cricket shot I ever played. I was facing a quick bowler of the Lansdown Cricket Club in Bristol. It looked like he had sent one down the leg side. I drew my feet together, looking to clip it off my legs down to the fine-leg area. But it was a full-length ball and swung late to the off side. I opened up – I still don't know whether I went forward with my leading leg or backward with my trailing one – and hit cleanly through the ball, which went like a bullet to the mid-on boundary. I think it may have been the only time I ever successfully executed a perfect on-drive – the most difficult shot in the book of cricket. And it was more or less an accident. I had no idea what I was doing until after it was all over. At that moment, there was no distinction between what I was and what I did: I was embodied mind in action.

According to Baruch Spinoza, the seventeenth-century Dutch philosopher, to be free is to act in accordance with necessity. In a similar vein, Taoism identifies freedom with *wu wei*: acting without acting. In a high-velocity sport, when you're 'in the zone', you act without acting. What you do is a perfect match with what the situation requires. Your actions are in accordance with necessity; you do what must be done. This almost accidental shot I played when I was fifteen years old, that is the most free I've ever been on the cricket pitch. If Spinoza is right, perhaps I have never been freer than at that moment.

The classic midlife crisis is about freedom, but of a specific sort. Certainly, it is about escaping the cares of an adult life, a life that may be slowly grinding you into a fine dust. But the form this escape takes attempts to replicate the freedom of youth. It is all about youth, in the form of a younger woman, and speed in the form of a sports car. This freedom is about running from old age: it is about reproducing the high-velocity freedom of youth – the freedom of a life that is flying at you intent on mischief. This is the freedom of Spinoza, the freedom that comes from acting in accordance with necessity. The freedom embodied in running distance is very different – it is not the freedom of Spinoza, not the freedom of youth.

The freedom of Spinoza collapses the distinction between mind and body. Indeed, Spinoza thought of mind and body as merely two aspects of the same thing. But in the freedom of running distance, the distinction between mind and body is likely to be augmented rather than effaced. This, at least for me, always starts the same way. When I was training for this race, the early part of the long run would take me up Old Cutler Road, from SW 152nd Street to SW 104th Street. By the time I'd reached 120th, I would be having a little conversation with myself: 'Just get me to the corner of 104th – then you can walk for a while.' But who or what is this 'me' and who or what is this 'you'? Who is giving permission to whom? It is my body that is suffering, not my mind. The mind might proffer a little encouragement every now and then, supply a little pep talk or two, but fundamentally it is my body that will get me to 104th, not my mind. It certainly seems as if my mind is giving permission to my body – and how can this be unless my mind is distinct from my body? This is the intuition that set the seventeenth-century philosopher and mathematician René Descartes, 'the father of modern philosophy', on his way.

According to Descartes, the body, which for his purposes incorporates the brain, is a physical object, differing only in the details of its organization from other physical objects. But the mind – or soul, or spirit, or self, Descartes was comfortable thinking of these interchangeably – is very different. The mind is a non-physical thing, composed of a different substance and obeying different laws and principles of operation than physical things. The resulting view – Cartesian dualism – sees each one of us as an amalgam of two very different things: a physical body and a non-physical mind. It is very unlikely that Descartes' view of the mind is correct.

Nevertheless, the most obvious freedom of the long run is the sort of freedom envisaged by Descartes rather than Spinoza. It is the flesh that is weak. The key to building distance in the long run is the ability of the mind to lie to the body – and be convincing. When we reach 104th Street, we must continue on. I must make sure my body is still putting one foot in front of the other at the steady pace I have set. The successful running spirit is sometimes, of necessity, a mendacious one. Self-deception lies at the heart of endurance.

There is so much more to the freedom of running than this. This Cartesian phase, where one lies to one's body and so seemingly – but presumably erroneously – demonstrates one's distinctness from it, is just the first phase, the first *face*, of freedom. There is another, entirely more interesting face to unveil: an old friend of mine whom I shall meet again today, assuming I last long enough. But without wishing to endorse Descartes' more general views of the relation between mind and body, it still seems true that whereas the freedom of youth effaces the difference between mind and body, the freedom of running distance accentuates it. The freedom of Spinoza is the freedom of youth. What do we say of the freedom of Descartes? How do we characterize it? Cicero, the ancient Roman philosopher, once said that to be a philosopher is to learn how to die. Cicero was a dualist in roughly the same sense as Descartes. The mind or spirit is a non-physical substance, and it survives the death of the body. According to Cicero, a philosopher is someone who knows how to die to the extent that he or she is someone who knows how to spend time with the mind – the part that, Cicero thought, survives death. A distance runner knows how to spend time with the mind – whether it does or, more likely, does not survive death. To run distance is not to run from old age; it is to run towards it. Far from a crisis, it is an acceptance of the point one has reached in life. And so the freedom of running distance is, it seems, the freedom of age. Far from reclaiming the freedom of youth, the freedom of distance running involves claiming, perhaps for the first time, an entirely different sort of freedom.

I'm still in corral G. Some men, local politicians of some sort I gather, are giving speeches now over a rather indistinct loudspeaker: 'You've trained for this for months, you've missed lunches, you've missed dinners, you've missed meetings . . .' Yeah, I wish I had. I continue to distract myself from my worrying lack of preparation with some further rumination on the nature of the midlife crisis, and the sort of thing it would have to be to explain why I am doing this. I think there is a type of freedom that is embodied in running distance, but not the sort of freedom embodied in youth, not my youth anyway. So it can hardly be a matter of reclaiming the freedom of youth. But, still, there is something in the idea of reclaiming that strikes me as correct and important. Running distance, I have come to suspect, is about trying to reclaim something from my youth. But, I have come to think, it is not freedom that is reclaimed: it is knowledge. That is the transformation I have been trying to identify.

Once upon a time, I knew something – something that I later forgot in the business of growing up. I didn't just forget it: I had to forget it – forgetting was part of the great game of becoming someone. I knew value. I did not know that I knew this, of course. But I knew it nonetheless. Caught up in the game of becoming, at first I didn't understand what I had lost in this forgetting. But, slowly, I came to feel this loss, and after that taste it: an aching in the bones and then a sourness in the blood. Running distance brings me back to what I once knew.

Most people who are not philosophers think that most people who are philosophers spend most of their time thinking about the meaning of life. But, as an example of the sort of historical irony that has characterized the development of philosophy in the last three centuries, that is precisely what philosophers do not do – not any more. Some of us may think about it, in our quieter moments, but we tend to keep it to ourselves. The meaning of life – that is something for a simpler time. We have moved beyond all that. Now we spend our time talking about things that cannot possibly be understood by anyone who has not had an extended formal training in philosophy. Philosophy has, in other words, become professionalized: it is a way of keeping out the riff-raff. When it comes to our own lives we are, as Julian Barnes once pointed out, all amateurs. And so the question of the meaning of life smacks of the sort of lack of professionalism that philosophers have tried to excise on the path to becoming a mature discipline. I am not endorsing any of these ideas – far from it – merely recording them. Thankfully, in the last decade or so, I sense attitudes are changing, the question is no longer necessarily taboo, even for the most dyed-in-the-wool professionals. But this is the way it has been for a long time.

Sentences have meaning; life is not a sentence; therefore life does not have meaning. Once upon a time, when philosophers had become so weary of philosophy they had come to hate it, they tried to get rid of philosophical problems rather than solve them. These philosophers thought that the claim that life is not a sentence was important. But in reality, of course, someone who asks 'What is the meaning of life?' doesn't really think that life has a meaning in the way that a sentence does. To ask 'What is the meaning of life?' is a way of asking another question: what is important in life? The question of meaning is a question of significance – not in the sense of semantic content but, rather, in the sense of importance. What is valuable in life? What makes life worth living? How should I live? – that is another way of asking the question, on the assumption that the way I live should reflect what I regard as important in life.

The use of the definite article in the question 'What is the meaning of life?' suggests that we are trying to find one thing that will answer the question – a miraculous truth in the light of which everything will make sense. But when we replace this question with its alternative form, 'What is important in life?', this presumption disappears. A nihilist might answer: nothing – although I suspect few nihilists ever really believe themselves. A more plausible answer is: there are many things that are important in life. Perhaps what these are will vary from person to person – what is important in life is, in this way, relative. But this merely raises another question. What is it for something to be important – whether for you, for me or someone else? And this is just a way of asking: what is value? What does it mean for something to have value?

The questions are the hard part. To even see that there is a question – there is the hardness, the difficulty, of philosophy. The answers: they are a mixed bag. It is rare for them to be unutterably complex or fiendishly difficult. On the contrary, Wittgenstein once claimed that the problem with philosophical truths is that, once you state them, they are so obvious that no one could ever doubt them. I think this claim is, to some extent, correct. But – and this is the strangest thing about the answers to philosophical questions – their banality is no guarantee of their intelligibility. To understand a philosophical answer, you need to understand how to work it out yourself. To do that, you need to see where it comes from.

You need to understand the force and urgency of the problem to which the answer is a solution; you need to understand the allure of the alternative solutions to this problem, and perhaps have succumbed to one or more of these alternative solutions at some point. In this respect, philosophical answers are utterly unlike the answers of any other domain of human knowledge or inquiry. If someone tells me that $E = mc^2$, for example, I might say, 'Thank you very much; I now know that the energy contained in a body is the product of its mass and the square of the speed of light.' To understand it, I do not need to know how to derive this equation – which is fortunate, as I haven't the faintest idea. Philosophical answers are not like this. Unless you know how to work them out, you will not really understand them.

When the philosophical question is a question about life – about what is important or valuable in life – the power and urgency of the problem is something that you have to feel in your life. The allure of alternative solutions to the problems, the succumbing to this allure, these are things you feel and do in your life and not, fundamentally, in your head. Unless you can feel the problem of the meaning of life – the problem of value in life – you will not understand any answer that might be given to it.

In the end, it is not in our minds that this answer is to be found. It is in our blood and bones that we understand value. It is only through living that you feel the problem of life's meaning. Through living you come to understand what life has in store for you. You understand this not just intellectually; you feel it viscerally, you taste it, an aching in the bones and a sourness in the blood. An answer to the question of what is valuable in life would tell us what redeems this life – what makes it worth living. To understand redemption in life, you need to understand from what, precisely, life needs redeeming. This is what you understand when you feel yourself growing old, feel your blood become thin and cool, feel your physical and intellectual powers begin to slide. If there is a meaning in this life, there is something that makes it, as Albert Camus once put it, 'worth the trouble'. That is why the question of the meaning of life – of value in life – is the most important question there is.

There is a Platonic dialogue – *The Meno* – in which Plato teaches a slave boy, the eponymous Meno, some of the theorems of Euclidean geometry. Plato argues that he has not taught Meno anything new, but merely helped him remember something that he once knew but had forgotten. We are all born with this sort of knowledge, Plato claimed, but forget it because of the trauma of birth. 'Anamnesis' is the name he used for this process of remembering what we once knew. For Plato, the idea of anamnesis was bound up with the Pythagorean idea of reincarnation, and I certainly do not believe in that. But the systematic forgetting of some of the most important truths, I think, is real. It happens not when we are born, but as we grow up. Any child knows value – they know what is important in life – although they do not know that they know it. And they know it in the way children know things, a kind of knowing that the adult finds very difficult, and has to learn all over again. Once I knew value. I knew it in my body and not in my mind, and so I did not know that I knew it. Running takes me back to this thing that I once knew but had to forget. Running puts me in contact once more with a certain kind of value that is easily lost to the adult. Running is a way of remembering – a way that the body remembers what the mind could not.

*

On the long run, there is an experience of freedom, of a certain sort – the freedom of spending time with the mind. On the long run, also, there is a certain type of knowledge: a kind of knowing that once permeated the lilting days of a life that was still young. This is knowledge of value, of what is important in life and what is not. The experience of freedom I find on the long run is not the experience of being able to do whatever I want. It is not the freedom that goes with absence of constraint. On the contrary, one of the things the long run teaches me is just how far I am removed from freedom in this sense. There is, however, another kind of freedom: a freedom that goes with knowing, a freedom that accompanies the absence of doubt.

The speeches are over. There is the gun, and we go ... absolutely nowhere. We're ten thousand back, and it'll take almost ten minutes for us to get across the starting line. A cheerful older gentleman who has been standing next to me in the corral, who told me his goal time was two hours – I did a double take until I realized he was running the half marathon not the full – whips off his tracksuit top and throws it backwards over his head into the crowd. He turns around to watch the result of this, and cackles when he sees, in the meagre light afforded us by the streetlamps, the confusion of the person on whom it has landed. So that's how you stay warm: you bring clothing with you that you don't plan on ever seeing again – next year, maybe. There is a lot of hooting, hollering, yipping and possibly even a little yodelling. We start moving forward. There is a shuffling walk, which slowly, almost imperceptibly, turns into a scuffling jog.

At some, perhaps not entirely determinate, point in this process, we shall find what we might think of as my first step in my first marathon. Here it is – I push off on my left foot and as I do, I find myself thinking: that is it. It has begun. That is the magical thing about first steps. Before that step I was outwardly calm but inwardly riddled with doubt: psychologically, a shifting, wriggling frame of confusion and uncertainty. Will my calf hold together? Will I be able to go the distance? How painful will this be? How humiliating? But with that first step, all my doubts are washed away by the quiet calm of certitude. According to Descartes, and a tradition instigated by him, to know something is to be certain of it, to have no doubts about it. We sometimes talk of being 'free of doubt', and I think there is a deep truth contained in this expression. Freedom and knowledge are closely entwined. The calm, quiet certitude that washes over me as I take this first step is the experiential form of a certain kind of knowledge. If I were more influenced by Spinoza, as I was when I was a younger man (and who, when they are young, could fail to be influenced by Spinoza?), then I might have been tempted to describe this understanding as the knowledge of how things have to be, of how things must be. But that would not be quite correct. Even as I take this step, I understand all too well that things did not have to be this way. My certitude consists in an understanding of how things should be rather than how they must be. But 'should' is a value term: a term that prescribes rather than describes. The experience of how things should be is an experience of value: an experience of what is important and, correlatively, implicit in the experience, an understanding of what is not. When the terror of doubt and indecision turns to calm, quiet, certainty, this is grounded in an experience of value.

As I take this first step, I understand that whatever happens today, however far I get, I should be here. I am doing what I should be doing. The experience of freedom I find on the long run is, in fact, the experience of a kind of value that I once knew but came to forget. Running is the embodied apprehension of this value. The first step is taken. The long run begins. I hope.

2

The Stone Mountain
1976

I have a dream of myself as an old man. I'm in a house, and I have the feeling that I am packing up to sell. Through the years, the house has been progressively decorated in new styles, but at least one room has always been left as a souvenir of the previous vogue. One room is 1970s chunky teak and padded beige; another is 1980s pine and sleek tubular steel. The 1990s room bears the indelible stamp of IKEA. It seems to me so improbable that all these things should belong in the same house. Rooting through the long-neglected attic I come across a collection of photographs that I cannot remember taking. The photographs depict people and places that seem vaguely familiar, but no more than that. I suspect the photographs are mine. In fact, I am pretty sure they are. I live in this house alone. Whose photographs would they be if not mine? But when I turn these photographs over, there is nothing written there that tells me to whom they belong. On the question of ownership, it seems that reasonable inference is the best I can do.

It is life itself I can't quite get: life in its breadth and depth. The longer I live, the more incongruous it all seems: the more trouble I have finding a place for everything – the more unlikely it seems that all these things should go together. Life progressively transforms itself from the natural and obvious to the gerrymandered and improbable. These memories I have, the ones that so enthusiastically thrust themselves upon me – they are mine. I have no doubt of that. It's my mind, and I'm the only one here: whose memories would they be if not mine? Possession is, after all, nine-tenths of the law. I'm not insane. I do not believe these memories were implanted in me by aliens. But there is nothing brightly embossed on them that reads 'Property of Mark Rowlands'. What strikes me as obvious is not that they are my memories, but that they couldn't be the memories of anyone else. Sometimes, this is the best I can do.

Remembering is effortless in its early days. There is so much room for each new memory, and no design or fashion exigencies to satisfy. But when the house of memory starts to become cluttered, then more and more remembering becomes an act of will, one that is sometimes difficult to execute with any real satisfaction. More and more the coherence – the sense – of a life is not something that is simply given but something that has to be achieved through one or another ad hoc manoeuvre. Memories, I suspect, disappear not because we can't make them any more – and not even because we no longer have room for them. They just become too incongruous, too unlikely. Perhaps, in the end, it will be my utter implausibility that does for me. I shall have become too improbable to be here any more – a hypothesis that can no longer be believed.

And so, from time to time but more and more, my attempts

to remember are characterized by a strange sense of amaze-ment. That these memories should all belong to a single life is a faintly surreal discovery. It strikes me as so extraordinar-ily unlikely – a fortuitous bonus – that they should all go together, bundled up in a single winding pathway through space and time. Was it really me that saw those things; that did those things? Even worse: I know enough about memory to know that the photograph model is deeply flawed. Memories are not replicas of past events. They are render-ings: part replica, part fabrication. A memory is an artifice stitched together by me. I am not just the cameraman, but the editor, and often the CGI man too. According to a well-known philosophical theory, I am my memories. It is my memories that make me the person I am today, a person different from anyone else. But I suspect you will not find me in my mem-ories at all – not in the content of those memories anyway. I am there only in the stitching, the splicing, only in the imagery I generate.

So what should I say of my memories of this day? The German poet Rainer Maria Rilke once wrote that the most important memories are the ones that become part of your blood. The blood of memory is not what is remembered but a way or style of remembering and, I suspect, I am to be found less and less in what I remember and more and more in a style of remembering.

Mynydd Maen – 'the mountain of stone' – divides the eastern and western valleys of Gwent. It is, in fact, barely a moun-tain, creeping just a little over 1500 feet. But on a good day you can see all the way to England: Bristol is a twinkle to the south, clinging to the far shore of the Channel. To the north you'll see the Black Mountains, the Sugar Loaf – Pen-y-Fal –

and the Blorenge; and beyond them, if the air is exceptionally clear, the Beacons. They are called the 'black' mountains, but this name is ironic. Most of the time, they are green, turning brown in autumn when the heather dies. The real black mountains lie before them. When I was a boy, the dark residue of the Industrial Revolution clung to everything. The hills were almost uniformly black, covered, steeped, in coal dust. Indeed, some were hills of coal not earth – mountains of coal slag. These mountains would often catch fire, deep inside them, and these fires could burn for years. There was no way of putting them out. We had family in a town called Nantyglo – 'the stream of coal' – and one Sunday a month we would drive up the valley to visit them. Climbing over a thousand feet through Blaenavon, on through the tiny coal-stained village of Garn-yr-erw, I would be sitting in the back of the car with my brother. Sheer black hillsides glowered down on either side of us, dark coal smoke billowing slowly from them. The poet Idris Davies once wrote, of mountains very much like these, that he could 'dream of the beauty lost and the beauty yet to be'. But it never occurred to me that this was unusual, that an artist might use such a scape to portray hell. It never occurred to me that this is what the end of the world might look like.

Mynydd Maen marked the point where the eastern valley opened out into coastal plain. There was little coal here, and so it had been spared the worst excesses of that brutal century. I am standing on, surrounded on all sides by, green mountain grass. To the south-east is Newport, where I was born. To the east is Cwmbran – 'the valley of the crow', a scabrous new town – where I am growing. The west – you can't see that – not from where I am standing today. The mountain ridge is a broad one. I'd spent quite a bit of time on this mountain, and I knew the geography of the land to the north and south and east like the back of my hand. But the west was still a mystery to me.

This was a morning alive, wriggling, with possibilities in a way that is true only of the mornings of youth: a fine, powdery dusting of prospects, options, risks and opportunities. It must have been late spring or early summer. That is the best my memory can do in locating this day in time. But I know it was a Saturday, and I remember that school was still in session. So May or perhaps early June would be my best guess. If it had been April, the mountain would still have been frosted white at this time of the morning.

The Saturdays of my childhood were largely filled with the playing of sports. Sometimes these were the formal team sports of my school, mostly rugby and cricket, and if by any chance there was a Saturday where there was nothing formal arranged, my friends and I would fill it with informal pick-up games of soccer. Free Saturdays – Saturdays when there was absolutely, positively nothing arranged – were few and far between, and if one did materialize, the chances were I just wanted to take off on my own. Or not quite on my own – flying out of the door with me this morning, breakfast barely settled in our two stomachs, is Boots, the huge, pale, almost white, Labrador of my childhood. We started walking: down Chapel Lane, past the Bluebell Woods, Boots bouncing along beside me. I decided to start running, a steady jog. I wouldn't say I had been a fat kid, but I was far from svelte – fattish wouldn't be far from the truth. But this last year or two had seen me lengthen, and thin out, dramatically, like a chubby wad of liquorice pulled out into a string. If I had known that was the last of the lengthening I was going to do, I might have cherished it even more.

That's the way life goes sometimes. But on this day I remember our shadows. Boots – a squat ball of muscular energy. I, my profile newly effaced and elongated, projected onto the rooted and stony banks that ran beside us; my newly long hair – a triumph of deposition over my mother's thirteen-year reign of short-back-and-sides terror – bouncing in the sun to the beat of my stride.

I ran, and Boots ran, not for any real reason: you don't need reasons to run when you are a kid or a dog. Then, running is a perfectly reasonable option for transporting yourself from one place to another. You no more need a reason for running than you need one for walking. Indeed, sometimes it is positively uncomfortable not to run. My life was a patchwork of events, occasions and obligations, and running was the thread that held it all together. School was a mile and a half away: I would run there in the morning and run home in the evening. Sometimes I'd make the round trip at lunchtime too. That was already six miles; and it didn't even occur to me to think of it as exercise. After school, three nights a week, was rugby training: two hours spent largely running. Then I'd run home to eat, do my homework and after that the hour of enforced piano practice insisted upon by my mother – a necessary counterbalance to the thuggery of the rest of my life, as she saw it. On Monday nights, when there was no rugby, I would sometimes run down to the boxing club for some training. When I arrived, they would usually send me out on a five-mile run. There would be a school rugby match most Saturday mornings in winter. And in the afternoons, I'd sometimes pick up a game with the youth team, run by the local rugby club. When summer came, things were slightly different. I'd play cricket for the local club instead of rugby for the school. There was less running involved. But I was a batting all-rounder, so there was still running aplenty, and club cricket took up all the weekend rather than just Saturday.

Things are different now, and the world is a different place. I gather that kids are driven to school, and they play computer games when they get home. I suspect I would have been climbing the walls if I had grown up today – a 'problem child'. There is a certain type of boy – I can't speak for girls, but I don't immediately see why they should be fundamentally different – who needs to run. And if he doesn't, then life is going to be a painful and confusing place. I was a boy like that.

To reach the top of Mynydd Maen – crowned with a tall radio mast – involved a steep, steep climb, in parts a scramble, of around three miles. When Boots and I arrived there, I was astonished to see my watch telling me that it had taken barely over half an hour. Even now, I think I must have got it wrong. Perhaps we set out earlier than I remembered? But, whatever the truth of the matter, when we arrived there, we just kept running, because it never occurred to us to stop.

The mountain-top was by no stretch of the imagination a treacherous one. There was the occasional sheer drop, and a few bogs sprinkled around. So you had to take care. But I knew this mountain well. I'd not brought water, but there was no need. You wouldn't want to drink from the brooks. Mortality among mountain sheep is high, and if you drank from a brook, there was a more than negligible chance you'd find a dead one in the water further upstream. But I knew where the springs were; where crystal-clear, ice-cold water bubbled magically out of the ground. Me first, then Boots: I didn't fancy the slobber. Boots and I kept running.

This was a little hard on the dog, you might think. Boots was no longer young. He would have been around eight years old at this time, and that is getting on a bit for a big-boned Lab. But as the children of yesterday spent their lives running, so too did their dogs. I had no worries about Boots. For two hours or so of every weekday evening of summer – when the demands of rugby and boxing had gone into their seasonal hiatus – we would play cricket. Bat in hand, I'd throw a ball – a hard, bouncy power ball was ideal – against the garage wall, and Boots would chase it off my bat and then bring it back to me. The grass beneath my feet had worn away to a dusty dirt patch. The ball, sopping wet from Boots's saliva, picked up the dirt, and the wall, once gleaming white, had slowly transformed over the years to near pitch-black. Two hours every summer evening of chasing; hunting down the ball, and only reluctantly being coaxed back into the house when it was too dark to see any more. Boots could run all day. And apparently, on this day, so could I. On we ran, tramping the wiry mountain grass and springy heather.

A couple of hours later, we arrived at Twmbarlwm – the remains of an Iron Age fort that once stood guard over the hills that gaze down on where Newport is today. All that remains of the fort is a conspicuous mound of earth on the ridge of the mountain-top, clothed with thin grass. Later in life, whenever I arrived back to visit my mum and dad, I would see Twmbarlwm – 'the tump' – as the train pulled into Newport, or later as I drove down the M4, letting me know that I had come home.

Then, we turned around and ran back because we still couldn't think of any reason not to. We arrived home from our day on the mountain at the beginning of the long twilight, in time for supper.

'Where did you go today?' asks my mum.

'Just up the mountain.'

I didn't bother to add that we had run the better part of a marathon. Boots was soon pestering me for an evening game of cricket – before it got too dark.

In some respects, this day anticipated certain themes that would dominate the runs of my later life. But in other respects, it was entirely unusual. The way I remember this day, it makes me sound like I was the Haile Gebrselassie – the great Ethiopian distance runner – of the eastern valley. But I really wasn't very good at running, not compared to many of my friends. I may have spent a large portion of my young life running places, but so did they. And many of them were much better at it than I was. I remember well the unqualified ignominy of my first cross-country run. This was an annual school event, and my first one took place only a year or so before this run along the Mynydd Maen. To describe myself as a jock would, probably, be anachronistic – the expression certainly hadn't reached the shores of Britain at this time. But I suppose that is what I was, anachronistically or not. A central figure in the rugby team, and captain of the cricket team, I'd expected to do well in this race – I don't remember how long it was, but somewhere around five miles would be my guess. But little skinny kids, some of whom were my friends, some of whom I barely knew – but all of whom were not fit to lace my rugby boots – blew by me as if I were standing still. I finished in the middle of the pack – and that is only if we assume the pack had a large middle. As a consequence, I developed something of a love-hate relationship with running. I still did it all the time, of course. Running to school day in day out, or even running with Boots on that mountain,

I never regarded as running. It was just part of life. But events – races – I did my best to steer well clear of those.

At least, I steered clear of them if they were above a certain distance. I did not mind the short stuff, largely because I was moderately good at it. I was on the track team in high school. That wasn't quite right either. 'Track team' is also a transatlanticism that seems to have insinuated itself into my thought patterns. We didn't have 'track teams' in south-east Wales in the 1970s. If there was a schools' athletics event coming up at the weekend, one of the sports teachers would say something like: 'Rowlands, you're quite fast. Go to the stadium on Saturday and run in the hundred metres.' Not fancying a Saturday spent hanging around the stadium waiting for my race, I would reply with something like:

'What about Parkesy, sir? He's faster than me.'

'He is away this weekend – you'll have to do it.'

Cwmbran had an athletics stadium – incongruously well equipped, given the ill-equipped state of Cwmbran as a whole. As a result, most athletics events in Wales were held there. So that is where I unenthusiastically found myself two or three weekends a year. I seem to remember I was once placed third in the Wales Under-15s One Hundred Metres Final – though I suspect there were lots of David Parkes' missing that day.

The hundred metres was my, somewhat reluctant, speciality. And that's only because there were not any shorter events on offer. I could do the two hundred metres at a pinch, but never the four hundred – in my view, that's an event reserved exclusively for masochists of the most twisted kind. You have to run pretty much as fast as you can for four hundred metres! How anyone could enjoy that is beyond me. Even the hundred was far too long for me, really.

I'm Mr Fast-Twitch. I'm at my best for the first five metres or so, and after that it all starts falling apart. If there was an Olympic event called 'Out of the Blocks', I'm convinced I could have gone a long way (to the extent it makes sense to talk of 'going a long way' in such an event).

In *Why We Run*, Bernd Heinrich, one of a vanishingly small number of people who managed to combine being a world-class biologist and a world-class distance runner, outlined the general anatomical characteristics of someone suited to distance running: 'Distance runners have one common trait – the good ones are skinny. The distance runner must fairly float along the ground, sometimes for hours on end. Ideally, he has light, thin bones, and long, thinly muscled legs, like a bird.' If that is the distance runner, then I am the anti-distance runner. I don't float, I thud (I have what's known as a very hard strike – apparently it's a problem, the source of many injuries down the years). I am far from bird-like. I have short legs, big bones and I'm broad. I like to think of myself as a mesomorph with endomorphic tendencies. More realistically, I am probably an endomorph with mesomorphic tendencies – assuming there is a difference between the two. At my best, if I'm training hard, I'm big and heavily muscled like a sprinter. At my worst, I'm a fat boy.

There are two basic types of muscle fibre – slow-twitch and fast-twitch. The successful distance runner's leg muscles are made of between 79 and 95 per cent of slow-twitch muscle fibres. The muscles of an average person's leg contain a fifty-fifty split of fast- and slow-twitch fibres. For an elite sprinter, the ratio is more like 25 per cent slow-twitch against 75 per cent fast-twitch fibres. Slow-twitch fibres burn fat, and can operate only with a continuous supply of oxygen. They work aerobically. Fast-twitch fibres burn glucose and operate without oxygen. That is, they operate anaerobically. The lactic burn you get in your legs when you sprint is the by-product of the anaerobic operation of your fast-twitch fibres.

The way you exercise has been shown to have a small effect on the ratio of slow- and fast-twitch muscle fibres. Gollnick and colleagues, in a classic 1972 study, suggested that rigorous aerobic exercise – he had his subjects run on a treadmill for one hour a day for four days a week for five months at 85–90 per cent of their maximum aerobic capacity (talk about earning your volunteer research subject stipend!) – could, at most, result in a 4 per cent rewiring of fast-twitch to slow-twitch fibres. This figure has been more or less borne out by subsequent studies.

Fast-twitch muscle fibres have, more recently, been discovered to divide into two sorts: FTa and FTb. FTa fibres have some of the characteristics of slow-twitch fibres. As fast-twitch fibres, they can work anaerobically, by burning glucose but, like slow-twitch fibres, they can work by burning oxygen too. The average person's fast-twitch fibres are split evenly, roughly 50 per cent of each sort. Hard and consistent exercise is more effective in transforming FTb into FTa fibres than it is in transforming fast-twitch into slow-twitch. Elite marathoners end up having almost no FTb fibres. I'm pretty sure that is not something I could emulate. More than that, I'm not sure I would want to.

So I suppose the most important and obvious fact about me as a distance runner is this: I am not very good at it. I have little aptitude for it, and I suspect this lack of aptitude is grounded in certain features of my biological make-up. I don't know what happened that day on Mynydd Maen. Then, I could not, for the life of me, see any reason why my legs should stop doing what they were doing – why they couldn't keep going like this all day and through the night. But no matter how much I would like to, no matter how much I've worked and trained to do just this, I have never since quite been able to replicate the sense of freedom and power that I felt that day on the mountain of stone when I was somewhere between a boy and a man.

I suspect the iron bonds of inevitability hold us all, young or old. But when we are young, and on our good days can barely contain the power that sings inside of us, our chains seem so much lighter. I ran that day with the freedom of youth, a freedom that could think of no reasons to stop, and so for which there were indeed no reasons. The freedom of youth is the freedom of a life that is overflowing, of a power that can only with difficulty be contained within the bodily vessel. When you grow older, this feeling inhabits you less and less. You come to understand all too well that there are many, many reasons to stop: reasons that thrust themselves upon you vociferously – and the more tired you become, the more insistent are these reasons. But if you are lucky, if you are very lucky, you will one day come to understand that these reasons – no matter how savagely they snarl – have no authority over you. That is the freedom of age.

The appeal to bodily constitution – bodily 'facticity' as the French existentialist philosophers sometimes designate it – is it perhaps just an excuse? After all, I've never had a muscle biopsy done. Perhaps if I did I would be staggered to learn that I have the muscle constitution of a world-class distance runner, 80 per cent slow-twitch fibres with virtually no FTbs. But I doubt it. Connected with my lack of biological aptitude is another feature of that day's run that became a recurring theme of the runs of later life: it was completely unplanned.

When I woke up that morning, I felt like taking off for the day with Boots, that's all. I didn't plan to run up the mountain. I didn't even know I was going to the mountain. I simply found myself running there. Sometimes I say I don't like running. Sometimes I believe it too. But I doubt this can really be accurate. I've been doing it for so long that, on some level at least, I suppose I must like it. But it is certainly true that I hated the thought of running. Until very recently at least – things have changed now, and there are reasons for this – if I wanted to go running, I had to make sure I didn't think I was going to go running. I had to sneak up on my runs.

If you read running magazines, they'll sometimes offer advice on how to motivate yourself to go running when you don't feel like it. For the businessman or woman, for example, the advice is to schedule your runs like you schedule a meeting, and then feel proud afterwards as if it was a job well done. For me, for a very long time, there was only one way I could get myself to go running and that was to convince myself that I wasn't going running. There is a British film of the 1960s, *Village of the Damned*, based on the John Wyndham novel *The Midwich Cuckoos*. It is about some aliens who take the form of children. They have some rather nasty telepathic powers and apparently plan to take over the world – the usual alien stuff. At the denouement, the hero, who has planted a bomb, is being telepathically probed by the alien children, who suspect he is up to something but are not quite sure what. He must, at all costs, not think of the bomb. That is how I used to approach my running. No, I'm definitely not going running today: no sir, not a chance. I'll just sit here and write. And then I'm up in a flash, tearing across the room: shorts on, runners on and out the door, one or more canines in tow, before my body has a chance to realize what's

going on and put together the usual objections or obstacles –
a feeling of enormous lassitude is its usual strategy.

This hatred of the thought of running – not running, the
thought of running – continued through my twenties, thirties
and some of my forties. I'm very different now. Now I can't
wait to get out on the road. Perhaps it is because I now have
two young sons: and, believe me, compared to spending a few
hours with them – which, don't misunderstand me, I love
doing – running twenty miles is a relaxing break. Or perhaps
it's because I am starting to understand that, in all the
injuries, niggles and general persistent low-grade pain that
goes with the approaching half century, my life of running
does not necessarily stretch out into the indefinite future. I
have a sell-by date, stamped quite legibly on my dodgy knees,
a rather boorish Achilles tendon, a questionable back and
recidivist calf muscles. And in the light of this, I have come to
understand that running is not just something I do. It is not
even something to which I have a right. It is a privilege.

I run with dogs, not humans. That was the other feature of
the run that was to be reiterated in the years to come.
Humans run together for company, for encouragement, to
talk, to shoot the breeze, just to be together. These reasons are
entirely understandable and respectable ones. But they are
not my reasons.

People sometimes assess the quality of their runs in terms
of times, distances and also in more sophisticated ways: the
AIs – the number, duration and intensity of the aerobic inter-
vals they have inserted into the miles they have run; the
TUT – the total uphill time and so on. But, as far as I am concerned, times, distances, AIs, TUTs – these are all just
contingencies, incidentals. Every run has its own heartbeat;

the years have taught me this. The heartbeat of the run is the essence of the run, what the run really is. There, on an early summer's morning on the mountain of stone, the heartbeat was a gentle one. There was the gentle sinking of my feet into mountain grass and heather. There was the whispering rustle of the mountain breeze in the branches of the twisted, wind-hunched trees. And there was the gentle dance of skylarks in this breeze. Most of all there was Boots: the gentle pant-pant-pant of his breath and the quiet jingle-jingle-jingle of the tags that adorned his collar.

In my later life, people will sometimes ask me what I think about when I run. It's a reasonable question – especially given the profession I shall come to adopt – but, nonetheless, the wrong one. The question betrays a lack of understanding of what the run does. Any answers I could give would be pretty boring. 'Oh God, this hurts' is an increasingly common refrain. More generally, what I think will reflect what is going on in my life before the run begins. If I am happy, I shall think happy thoughts; if I am sad, I shall think sad ones. Thinking carries too much of me in it; too much of the stench of my life, its concerns and preoccupations.

If I am thinking at all when I run, this is a sign of a run gone wrong – or, at least, of a run that has not yet gone right. The run does not yet have me in its grip. I am not yet in the heartbeat of the run; the rhythm of the run has not done its hypnotic work. On every long run that has gone right, there comes a point where thinking stops and thoughts begin. Sometimes these are worthless, but sometimes they are not. Running is the open space where thoughts come to play. I do not run in order to think. But when I run, thoughts will come. These thoughts are not something external to the run – an additional bonus or pay-off that accompanies the run. They are a part of what it is to run, of what the run really is. When my body runs, my thoughts do too and in a way that has little to do with my devices or choosing.

There have been a number of studies on the effects running has on the brain – at least, the brains of mice – and these effects are quite impressive. Not so long ago, no one knew that adult neurogenesis – the growing of new brain cells as an adult – was even possible. But it seems that it is, and running is one of the things that can make it happen. At least it does in mice – when allowed free access to treadmills, laboratory mice grew hundreds of thousands of new cells in the hippocampus, a part of the brain associated with memory. Then there is BDNF – brain-derived neurotrophic factor. This is a protein that aids both in the formation of new brain cells and also in the protection of currently existing cells – and running produces lots of it. There may come a time when I am very happy about these effects that running has had on my brain, but for the present they do not concern me. I am more interested in what happens to my brain when I run, rather than afterwards. But until fMRI – functional magnetic resonance imaging – technology grows significantly more portable than it currently is, I shall probably not be able to find out, at least not directly. Nevertheless, I think it's possible to make reasonable extrapolations from work done on other aspects of brain function, particularly with regard to the connection between rhythm and information processing.

Let us begin with the phenomenon to be explained: the way it feels to you when you run. I described this in terms of a transformation of thinking into thoughts, and suggested that the hypnotic effect of rhythm was at the root of this transformation. If this phenomenon were unique to me, then it would be largely uninteresting (except to me, of course). But other people have described substantially similar experiences. For example, Joyce Carol Oates writes: 'Running! If there's any activity happier, more exhilarating, more nourishing to the imagination, I can't think of what it might be. In running the mind flees with the body, the mysterious efflorescence of language seems to pulse in the brain, in rhythm with our feet and the swinging of our arms.' And, in a similar vein, but with a slightly different emphasis, Haruki Murakami writes: 'When I am running my mind empties itself. Everything I think while running is subordinate to the process. The thoughts that impose themselves on me while running are like light gusts of wind – they appear all of a sudden, disappear again and change nothing.' Both Oates and Murakami identify important but different aspects of the experience. With Oates, the emphasis is on rhythm: the fleeing and pulsing of thought in tune with the swinging arms and moving feet. Murakami emphasizes the emptiness of the mind, and compares thoughts to gusts of wind that blow through this emptiness. I differ from Murakami in this respect: he claims that, for him, these thoughts change nothing. Sometimes that is true for me too. But occasionally, just occasionally, they can change everything. Then, rather than a feathery breath that gently caresses my cheek, they are more like a sharp slap.

Thoughts only come when they are ready. They cannot be forced, they cannot be hurried – they cannot be bargained with. They come in their time, not ours. In the many years that have come and gone since that day on Mynydd Maen, I have lost count of the number of times that a problem I have been trying to solve – and my business is hard, abstract, conceptual problems – has suddenly resolved itself, or if not that then dissolved before my eyes, during a run. Part of the explanation for this almost certainly lies in the idea of rhythm.

When someone taps out a regular rhythm, activation will occur in regions of the left frontal cortex, left parietal cortex and right cerebellum. Just as important as the location of this activity is its frequency. This frequency is in the gamma band: 25–100 Hz, but 40 Hz is typical. Gamma oscillations are thought by many to be the key to optimal information processing in the brain, underlying processes like attention and perhaps conscious experience. Some think this is because of the role gamma oscillations play in binding activity together into a unified whole. Francis Crick and Christof Koch famously argued that gamma oscillations of around 40 Hz are responsible for binding information together in visual awareness, and so are essential to visual experience – although this claim is controversial. Nevertheless, the idea that gamma oscillations are implicated in efficient cognitive performance is now largely accepted. In fact, the technique of optogenetics, developed by Karl Deisseroth's team at Stanford University, fairly conclusively demonstrates this. In optogenetics, one manipulates the rhythm of the brain through pulses of light directed at a type of neuron that produces parvalbumin – a type of protein that regulates the frequency of gamma wave oscillations in the brain. Using this technique, Deisseroth demonstrated that the right frequency of gamma oscillation will 'enhance information flow among cells in the frontal cortex'. The frontal cortex is the area of the brain associated with higher cognitive functions like thought.

It is notable that the optimal frequency of gamma oscillations – around 40 Hz – can be induced simply by tapping out a rhythm with one's finger. So it is not too much of a stretch to suppose that moving one's entire body in an appropriate rhythm can produce the same effect. Indeed, one might suspect that if tapping one's finger can induce the appropriate frequency of gamma oscillations, moving one's whole body might do this a little more forcefully. It is therefore not implausible that there is a connection between the rhythm of the body involved in running and the presence of the brain activity involved in higher cognitive functions. However, rhythm cannot be the whole story. Tapping my finger at a frequency of 40 Hz for hours on end would, at most, lead to a sore finger.

Wolfgang Ketterle, a Nobel-Prize-winning physicist at MIT, also notes the beneficial effect running has on his problem-solving abilities. He describes this effect in terms of the idea of relaxation: 'Some solutions are obvious, but they are only obvious when you are relaxed enough to find them.' But I don't think this is quite right – at least, that is not how it is for me. To begin with, to state the obvious, there are many ways of relaxing – I'm actually extraordinarily good at relaxing, especially if there's a TV, a comfortable sofa and a bottle of halfway decent wine in the vicinity. Unfortunately, the solutions to difficult conceptual problems do not seem to announce themselves when I am doing this. Since they are far more likely to appear when I am running, I have to conclude that exhaustion rather than relaxation must play at least some role. Up to a certain point – there is a point of exhaustion that is the death of thoughts – the longer the run goes on, the more tired I become, then the more likely it is that a solution will appear. But this will only work if the rhythm has been established first. It's not as if I can refrain from running for six months, start again, find myself feeling like death after two miles on my return, and expect all these worthy thoughts to appear as if from nowhere and solve all the problems I've been working on for those past months. It would be much easier if things happened like that, but they don't. On a run like that, I never get beyond thinking – usually badly: thoughts have no wish to be associated with me. The reason, I suppose, is that my mind will not be empty. For that I need the rhythm, and to get that I need to be in shape.

So it seems that, for me at least, there are two crucial factors: rhythm and exhaustion. Neither will work in isolation. Having less empirical work to fall back on, I have to be more speculative with regard to the effects of exhaustion on higher cognitive functions. First, there are some general principles about how the brain works which might be pertinent. The brain is a creature of habit. It travels down the same streets and avenues, visiting again and again the same old cul-de-sacs, dead ends and no through roads of thought. The reason is that the brain is, in essence, an associative machine. Activity spreads in the brain through associations. If activation in one area of the brain has, in the past, produced activation in another area, then an association between the two is set up, and this means that, in the future, when another instance of the first sort of activity occurs, it is more likely that activity of the second sort will occur too. The tendency of humans to make, both individually and collectively, the same mistakes in thinking over and over again – and even a cursory glance at the history of thought will show that essentially the same, typically unsuccessful, ideas are revisited over and over again, in slightly different forms – is a testament to the associative nature of the brain.

Sometimes, the brain has to be persuaded to let go, just for a while, and when it is tired it is perhaps more easily persuaded. When I talk to someone who suffers from dementia or Alzheimer's, I am often struck not so much by the extent of the memories they have lost, but of the power and vivacity of the ones that remain. Memories from a long time ago, from a lifetime ago, are uncovered once again, as if they were new-born moments before. Their brain is letting go, associations are breaking down and in this process we find the uncovering of things that were hidden. That, I suspect, is the sort of thing that happens when tiredness starts to insinuate its way into the rhythm of my run. Emptiness is the sign of the brain letting go – not letting go in general, but simply allowing its grip to loosen on its day-to-day executive duties. The associations through which its activity is channelled are loosened, just a little. And so, to an extent, the familiar but fruitless avenues and dead ends of thinking are left behind, and in this new desert landscape of the mind thoughts are uncovered, shining and pristine.

There is one piece of empirical work that bears specifically on this topic. In a study of Tibetan Buddhist monks, neuroscientist Sean O'Nuallain demonstrated a correlation between transcendental mental states and gamma wave oscillations of around 40 Hz. More than this, however, he also argued that what these monks have in common – at least the ones proficient at this sort of meditation – was the ability to put their brain into a state in which it consumes power at a lower rate than usual, sometimes approximating zero. According to his 'zero power hypothesis', lower power states of the brain may correspond to a selfless state, and higher power states correspond to the experience of the self. Gamma oscillations are more prevalent in lower power states.

This work is strongly suggestive of the role tiredness may play in thinking – or, more accurately, in the having of thoughts. Intense activity of the body results in the brain adopting a lower power state. The principle would be like feeling sleepy after a heavy meal. Blood has been diverted to the intestine to facilitate digestion, and as a result less blood, and therefore less oxygen, goes to the brain. On the long run, when you reach the point when you are struggling, all your energy must be directed to putting one foot in front of the other. To compensate, the brain – normally taking up more than 20 per cent of the body's total energy supply – goes into a lower power state in the way described by O'Nuallain. The result is a 'selfless' state. Thinking is typically something I experience myself as doing. On the long run, I don't experience myself to be thinking because the grip I have on myself has become more tenuous. In place of thinking, there are thoughts, seemingly not mine at all, that come from nowhere, out of the blue and into the black.

Thoughts come in their own good time – and this, I suspect, is what their own good time might look like: an increase in gamma activity coupled with a decrease in the overall power state of the brain. There is highly integrated activity in the left frontal cortex, left parietal cortex and right cerebellum, coupled with the kind of tiredness that allows the usual associations of daily life to break down just enough. The result is a kind of emptiness: a clearing in the mind where thoughts can come to play. Maybe that is why it happens, maybe not. But, for me, far more important than why this happens is that it does, in fact, happen.

Talk is antithetical to thought. And so I run with dogs that do not talk. But they do more than that. They augment: they magnify the rhythm, enhance the essence, of the run. My heartbeat is magnified by those of the dogs that run beside me; my breath is magnified by theirs. The thud-thud-thud of my feet is expanded and enhanced by the pitter-pitter-pitter-pat of theirs and the chingle-chingle-chingle of the chains around their necks. This is the heartbeat of the run, a heart that beats outside me, not within. And when the run has done its work, I am lost in this beating heart. Before this point, the point when thinking stops and thoughts begin, I am not running, not really. I am only moving. The point where movement transforms into running: that is the point at which thoughts come to play.

That day on Mynydd Maen was perhaps my first experience of the heartbeat of the run – the heart that beats outside me, not within. I could not have understood, neither then nor for many years to come, that this experience would come to shape my life in some of its more important respects. To experience the heartbeat of the run is to have one of the most powerful experiences possible of what Plato would have called 'The Good'. Many years will have to come and go before the heartbeat of the run will reacquaint me with a kind of value that the child knows best. The idea that life is the sort of thing that needs this value – that an adult who has lost it has become, in a significant sense, a diminished thing – is not something I could have known on that day when I ran with Boots on the mountain of stone, when thoughts that came from the beating heart of the run danced in the place my mind used to be, as the sun danced on the bright blue waters of the sea that lay to the south.

3

Born to Run
1999

Every run has its own heartbeat; the years are teaching me this. The heartbeat is the essence of the run, what the run really is; and the heart beats outside me, not within. Permeating everything is the backbeat: the gusty, undulating thunder of the wind in my ears. I am on the Rathmore Peninsula of Kinsale, slap bang in the middle of the southern coast of Ireland, and the wind accompanies every step I take: ebbing and flowing, never constant, whoosh, silence, whoosh, silence. Then there is the pack. I am running with Brenin, the wolf, Nina, his dog-friend, and Tess, his wolf-dog daughter. There is the pad-pad-pad of a dozen feet, the click-click-click of forty-eight claws, enamelled metronomes tapping out the beat of distance covered and time elapsed on the cracked, faded, potholed tarmac. There is the pant-pant-pant of three breaths and the jingle-jangle of three chains. These all fuse with the whoosh and the silence.

There are few cars on these narrow, crooked country lanes,

and I can let the pack run as it will. More or less: anywhere behind me, but nowhere in front. That is the rule. This is not a matter of dominance, simply safety. But, anyway, they fall into my rhythm, effortlessly ghosting over the ground beside me. Beyond that, it is fluid, always shifting. The flowered hedgerows that line the lanes, the towering hedgerows of summer, are teeming, fidgeting with life. A promising rustle, perhaps a mouse, shrew, rabbit or rat, draws out one of the pack – Brenin plunging paws first, canine hope personified, rigidified, into the buttercupped, cow-parsleyed under-growth, disappearing up to his tail – and then an empty-jawed return to the rhythm of the pack. This severance and return – to be repeated over and over again during the course of the run – is part of the heartbeat.

Now we are drawing close to the place where the rabbits live: around the corner, and four hundred strides to where the hedgerows open up into a field. Marking the entrance are two hulking, rotting bales of hay that have been here longer than we have. Between the bales is a rabbit warren, and today as ever, the rabbits will be making the most of the milky, ret-icent Irish summer sun. Reticent is about as good as the sun gets in these parts. As we turn the corner, I can feel the excitement of the pack beginning to build. We're still three hundred strides away, but they try to persuade me to run faster, slowly building the pressure. Brenin inches his nose in front of me, testing the water. 'Back!' I growl, but inwardly smile, gesticulating brusquely with my thumb. Seconds later, Nina tries the same thing. That was the strategy. First one animal then another: testing me. Another growl: 'Wait for it!' Then, an agony of moments later, I release the tension: 'Go on!' and we sprint the remaining distance. It's an enjoyable way of getting in some speed work. I need it. By the time I have reached the bales, trailing miserably behind the others, the pack has dissolved before my eyes: Brenin one way, Nina another, Tess yet another – a frenzy of chasing and snapping and slipping. To no avail – no rabbits were ever harmed on these runs. Perhaps they hear us thundering along the lane, and by the time we arrive are waiting, patient, unsurprised, maybe a little amused, by their burrows. I don't know. I'm hunched over, winded, often nauseous, but always elated. The pack bounces up to me in unison, tongues lolling, eyes shining with excitement: that was fun, maybe better luck tomorrow. A few minutes later, we are back on the road and the gentle rhythm of the pack reasserts itself.

When I was twenty-seven, I did something really rather stupid. Actually, I almost certainly did many stupid things that year, but this is the only one I remember because it went on to indelibly shape the future course of my life. When I first met – and acquired – Brenin, I was a young assistant professor of philosophy at the University of Alabama, and he was six weeks old, a cuddly little teddy bear of a wolf cub. At least, he was sold to me as a wolf, but it is quite likely that he was a wolf-dog mix. Whatever he was, he grew up.

On the following page is a picture of us taken some years after we left Alabama: taken, in fact, at a place we shall pass on today's run. This is at Charles Fort, in a little village called Summer Cove, a couple of miles outside Kinsale. As a result of having to live with a rootless and restless philosopher, Brenin became a very cosmopolitan wolf, moving with me from Alabama to Ireland, on to England and finally to France. At the time this photograph was taken, Brenin would have been around seven years old, and this day was my thirty-fifth birthday.

The first run I ever took with Brenin was short but not entirely without incident. I ran from the living room to the bedroom, to the study, to the next bedroom, to that other room I never knew what to do with, to the kitchen, to the den, and then out of, and finally under, the house. I was not so much running with Brenin as after him. I had bought him that day and was introducing him to the house. His first act was to rip down the curtains in every room, before finding an open back door. He then made his way out into the yard, and then, through another open door, managed to make his way under the house where he ripped down all the soft-lagged pipes leading the cold air from the air conditioner back into the house. $500 those two minutes cost me, to go with the $500 it had cost me to buy Brenin scarcely more than an hour before. In those days, that was nearly a twentieth of my annual salary.

A playful cub, you might think. But it's not as if he mellowed as he grew up. If anything, he got worse. Brenin had, let us say, certain idiosyncrasies. If I left him unattended for more than a few minutes, he would destroy anything he could lay his jaws on – which, given that he grew to be thirty-five inches at the withers, included pretty much everything that wasn't screwed to the ceiling. I don't know whether he was easily bored, had separation anxiety, or claustrophobia, or some combination of all of these things. But the result was that Brenin had to go everywhere I did. I took him to lectures with me. He would lie down and sleep in the corner of the lecture room: most of the time anyway – when he didn't, things would get interesting. Any socializing I did – bars, parties – he had to come too. If I had a date, he would play the lupine gooseberry. For more than a decade Brenin and I lived our lives in each other's pockets.

Allied to his destructive proclivities was his boundless energy. When Brenin was a cub, and then a young wolf, he liked to play a game: he would grab a cushion off the sofa or armchair on which I was sitting, and tear off out to the garden, with me in hot pursuit. It was a game of chase and he loved it. But when he started getting big, he decided to modify the game. One day, sitting in my study, my reflections were interrupted by a sequence of loud thuds coming from the room that led out to the back garden. Instead of taking a cushion from the armchair and going out to the garden, Brenin had decided that it would be far more rewarding to take the rest of the armchair too. The thuds were made by the chair, locked firmly in Brenin's jaws, being repeatedly slammed against the doorframe. I think it was at precisely this moment I decided that, all things considered, it would be a really good thing if Brenin were constantly exhausted. And so our daily walks together became daily runs. That is the how, when and why of the beginning of my life of running, at least as an adult. The years will see us move across an ocean. Our pack will double in size. But our running together started that day in Tuscaloosa, Alabama, with the thud-thud-thud of an armchair against a doorframe.

Aristotle claimed that anything that exists – object, person, event, state or process – has four causes. When he talked of 'causes', Aristotle meant something like what we would call an 'explanation'. Anything that exists – and my running is no exception – can be explained in four different ways. We need to understand all of these ways if we are to understand the thing in question. Brenin was what Aristotle would have called the efficient cause of my running. The efficient cause of something is its immediate impetus. When one billiard ball hits another – to use the sort of example philosophers typically employ in this context – and makes the second move, the movement of the first is the efficient cause of the movement of the second. Brenin, of boundless energy and destructive appetites whose limits I had no desire to test, was the efficient cause of my beginning to run, and the efficient cause of my continuing to run, day in day out, rain or shine.

When he was around four years of age, we moved from Alabama to County Cork, Ireland, where Brenin was soon joined by other efficient causes. Brenin had to go into quarantine for six months. This was back in the days before pet passports and the like, and the British and Irish governments apparently had not had time to catch up with the recent invention of a rabies vaccine by Louis Pasteur and Emile Roux in 1885. When he was released, I vowed to make the second half of his life as good as it could possibly be and so decided to get him a friend, one with more legs and a colder nose than I. The result was Nina, a German shepherd/Malamute

mix. Here she is, pictured in Knockduff Lodge, the tiny, drafty, tumbledown cottage we all shared. She's still quite a young dog (her muzzle went prematurely grey), and here she's in full-on 'take me for a run or I might just have to kill you' mode.

A couple of years after Nina had joined us, Brenin unilaterally decided to augment the pack on his own. An illicit rendezvous with a white German shepherd a few miles away resulted – sixty-three days plus around five weeks later – in the addition of Tess. She grew up to resemble her father in many ways. She was predominantly grey rather than brown, but you could certainly tell whose daughter she was. I remember her as a softer, gentler version of Brenin: a toy wolf, beautiful but just a little too round, a little too fluffy. She never quite acquired the clean angularity of her father and her coat was far less coarse. Just a smidgeon too cuddly to be a real wolf, Tess was elegant, retiring and she loved comfort. There wasn't an aggressive bone in her body. I once had to rescue her from a savaging at the hands of a Jack Russell. This was largely the result of Nina's unsparing efforts. Being the older dog, Nina was alpha female; and she intended to keep it that way. Any sign whatsoever of Tess asserting her authority would be ruthlessly stamped out by Nina. If she had fought back against the little terrier, Nina probably would have joined in – and not on Tess's side. Nonetheless, as you can see, they were the best of friends.

Here, Tess is around six months of age and still has a lot of growing to do. When she was fully grown, she was a little bit bigger than Nina. Everyone thought she was much smaller.

Both Nina and Tess seemed to worship Brenin – at least, they copied everything he did. This was far from an unadulterated blessing. Brenin would eat my house and all my possessions if I left him unattended. So you can imagine what the three of them could do together. Our daily runs continued with renewed urgency.

Brenin, Nina and Tess were the efficient causes of my beginning to run, and my continuing to run, every day – whatever the weather and whatever my state of health. Bad things would happen if I didn't. Serious illness, the loss of a limb or something like that, might have bought me a day's grace. But, after that, I'm sure they would have expected me to trundle around the lanes in a motorized wheelchair. Those animals needed to run, and would accept no excuses.

If Aristotle is right, however, there is more to understanding something than just its efficient cause. He writes:

'Cause' means: (a) in one sense, that as the result of whose presence something comes into being – e.g. the bronze of a statue and the silver of a cup; (b) in another sense, the form or pattern; that is, the essential formula and the classes which contain it; (c) the source of the first beginning of change or rest – e.g. the man who plans is a cause, and the father is the cause of the child, and in general that which produces is the cause of that which is produced, and that which changes of that which is changed; (d) the same as 'end'; i.e. the final cause – e.g. as the 'end' of walking is health.

Here, the idea of an efficient cause is captured by (c). Brenin, Nina and Tess were the efficient causes of my running, in the way that the father is the cause of the child. Or, in the case of a statue, one of Aristotle's favourite examples, the efficient cause would be the sculptor, chiselling away at a lump of marble. Brenin, and then Nina and Tess, were the sculptors of my running in this sense – chipping (or perhaps gnawing) away at the couch potato to reveal the runner underneath. But to understand the statue we need to understand more than this: we also need to understand what Aristotle called the 'material' and 'formal' causes of the statue. The material cause of the statue is the material from which it is made:

the lump of marble or whatever else the sculptor employs. The formal cause of the statue is its form or shape: what it is a statue of – a wolf, a dog, a man, etc. To understand something like a statue you need to understand not only who or what makes it (the efficient cause), but also from what it is made (the material cause) and what it is that is being made (the formal cause).

There are, of course, no runs in the abstract. There are just the runnings of runners, concrete episodes where a certain physical body changes its location, moves from A to B, in a certain way. Both the material and the formal cause of my running coalesce in me. The material cause is me: Mark Rowlands, lump of meat. The formal cause of my running is the way this meat has been organized. And what way is that, precisely?

Aristotle defined humans as rational animals. Echoing him, despite more than a little evidence to the contrary, we now refer to ourselves as *Homo sapiens*. Of course, we have every reason to be delighted with the way our cerebral cortex turned out. A very large and impressive cerebral cortex it is. On the other hand, we might, with approximately equal justification, focus on our large and impressive arses.

When I started running with Brenin, I suffered from a rather unfortunate case of species-envy. He would glide over the ground with a grace and economy of movement I could never match: from a distance it would look like he was floating an inch or two above the surface of the earth. I, on the other hand, was the clumsy featherless biped, the leaden-footed monkey puffing and thudding along beside him. I rail against this misfortune at some length in *The Philosopher and the Wolf*.

But, of course, it is all relative. I may not look good next to a wolf, but compared to other apes, I'm really not bad at it. By 'other apes' I mean non-human ones. Like most other humans, I am much better at running than my simian cousins. Playing a not insignificant role in my augmented abilities is my *gluteus maximus*. Gorillas, chimpanzees, orangutans – they never developed glutes, not big ones like I have. What distinguishes me from my simian brothers is the size of my arse. For entirely understandable reasons, we humans would rather focus on our cerebral cortex or, at a pinch, our extraordinarily flexible thumbs. But I think a good case can be made for the arse being the crowning bodily development of human beings – the decisive phenotypic modification that paved the way for everything else. It is our arses that allow us to run upright, instead of bumbling and stumbling along on our knuckles like other apes. It is all very well to come down from the trees, but without an arse there's really not much to do afterwards.

I am already at that age where if I do not run, my arse will disappear. My gut will get bigger and my arse will get flatter. I've been there. Then, big shouldered and somewhat hirsute, more and more I come to resemble a gorilla. When I don't run, I regress – at least in bodily terms – to the ape I would have been if evolution had never come up with big arses. Running is what keeps me in touch with what is distinctively human in me: my big-arsed humanity.

My constant companion – wherever I turn, my arse is there – is also a reminder of just how ill designed I am for the life I lead. Human beings – or at least their recognizable big-arsed precursors – first made an appearance in the fossil record about two million years ago. Agriculture didn't make an appearance until around 10,000 years ago. For the other 1.99 million years we were hunter-gatherers. If we think of the current span of the human race as twenty-four hours on a clock, then the modern sedentary me, the me who spends much of his day sitting and eats food grown and picked (and, in my earlier years, raised and killed) by someone else, was born no more than a few seconds before midnight.

According to Loren Cordain and colleagues, hunter-gatherer males typically expend around twenty to twenty-five kilocalories per kilogram of body weight per day in physical activity. A modern sedentary office worker typically expends less than five kilocalories per kilogram per day. If we introduce a three-kilometre walk into the office worker's day, this only ups the energy expenditure to less than nine kilocalories per kilogram per day. It is only when more vigorous forms of exercise are introduced – for example, a sixty-minute run at a pace of twelve kilometres per hour – that we start to reproduce the energy expenditure levels of our Stone Age ancestors.

We are, it goes without saying, the product of evolutionary processes. And evolution takes a long time to get things done. Even if it perhaps does not work as slowly as people used to think, 10,000 years, in evolutionary terms, is the blink of an eye. Any biological changes wrought in us in the last 10,000 years will be relatively minor. The inescapable conclusion seems to be that our modern sedentary life is one for which we have not been designed and for which, at least biologically, we are poorly equipped. It is a common misconception – pervasive and tenacious, but a misconception nonetheless – that arses are made for sitting on. It seems, instead, they are made for running. We are happiest and healthiest when we live our history, and so become what we are.

Beside me runs a living representation of this truth. We race down a steep lane that will swing around to the left and bring us to Charles Fort. This is a star-shaped fort built in the seventeenth century on the site, like so many things in Ireland, of something far older: Ringcurran Castle. The fort was on most of our running routes and marked the lowest point in this rollercoaster of a run. The south and west of its walls – the Cockpit Bastion and the Devil's – loom over us as we round the bend, and promise us a speedy turn, at least it might have been speedy if it had not involved climbing a frighteningly steep hill to the east and the start of the long road home to Knockduff.

I have to be careful on this descent. There is a Welsh proverb: *Henaint ni ddaw ei hunan* – old age doesn't come on its own. Lately, incipient old age has been consorting with some calf issues. Down a hill this steep, there is anywhere between seven and twelve times my body weight being put on each stride, and my left calf has already gone a couple of times in the past six months (I had to buy a mountain bike to exercise the beasts during my recuperations). Armed with new running shoes and new caution, my former charge down the hill has transformed into a careful plod. At the bottom of the hill, in the shadow of the Devil's Bastion, I relax, if that's the right word, and prepare for the climb home.

Nina has the markings of a shepherd, but the massive, muscled shoulders and barrel chest of a dog bred for pulling. She is in effect the result of a great split in the wolf nation that occurred, according to current estimates, between 15,000 and 30,000 years ago (yes, current estimates are that exact). The division came about through random mutation and natural selection. No one is really sure why it happened, but probably the most plausible story looks like this. Some wolves, as a result of simple genetic variation, developed a lower flight threshold distance. That is, they were more able than the average wolf to tolerate the proximity of these new, strange, big-arsed apes. As a result, as well as obvious dangers, they were also presented with certain opportunities that escaped their more cautious peers. These wolves started to specialize in the refuse of the apes. They became scavengers, not hunters. Some wolves learned early on that if you can't beat the big-arsed apes – and it turns out you can't – then you have to join them.

The rest is history, and a moment's thought is enough to convince us of just how incredibly successful this evolutionary strategy was: 400 million dogs on the planet compared to 400,000 wolves is pretty conclusive evidence. As a result of their new niche, dogs did undergo certain, relatively minor, phenotypic changes. Their heads became somewhat smaller in proportion to their body size: scavengers typically have smaller brains than hunters. But fundamentally the dog and the wolf are the same: 15–30,000 years is not enough time for evolution to finish its morning coffee, let alone fashion any decisive biological modifications. That is why, since 1993, wolves and dogs have been classified as the same species.

What use would a scavenger have for running – the sort of running we do together, the running of the pack? You can understand why short bursts of speed would be of use to a scavenger specializing in human refuse. Humans can be unpredictable. But what use would this mile after mile of metronomic trotting be to such a creature? But if it were no use to her kind, why does Nina love it so much? Why the blistering excitement, once we have hurried out of the door and she realizes what is happening?

You might think it is her breed. German shepherds were bred for herding, and Malamutes were bred for pulling sleds. There is a lot of running involved in both. This is true, but this can't be all that there is to it. This love of running is indifferent to breed. Unless the dog has been ruined by its human owner – and, admittedly, that is not uncommon – it is going to want to run. It doesn't matter whether it's a greyhound or a poodle, once it knows what running is, it is going to love doing it.

The real answer is that Nina and all other dogs are built on something much older. While she is, in some small part, what the last 15–30,000 years have made her, more than that, much more, she is what the preceding millions of years made her. Yes, she is happy when I feed her; and she likes her bed in front of the fire in our draughty cottage. But Nina is happiest when she is charging up that lane in search of rabbits. Nina is still fundamentally a wolf: she is at her happiest, and she is at her best, when she is doing wolfish things.

Nina and I are both built on something much older. I may be a rational animal, but I am therefore an animal. And the animal that I am is one that was made not by the last 10,000 years but by the millions of years that preceded them. Running with this pack is the clearest possible expression of my humanity: the perfect congruence of what I am and what I am supposed to be. Along these gusty, winding, plunging country lanes, with wolves and dogs, I am returned to the formal and material cause that I am: a big-arsed ape that has been designed to run.

The thoughts that join me on my runs – my other running companions – are not always entirely serious ones. That is not necessarily a bad thing. Sometimes the thoughts that are tinged with parody are the best ones to have, not because of what they tell me but because of what they show me. This is undoubtedly true of the big-arsed-ape hypothesis.

Explanations in terms of efficient, formal and material causes are all species of historical explanation. When the emphasis is on efficient causes, the history is very recent – the fruits of the destructive efforts of Brenin, Nina and Tess are events that litter my recent history. When the focus shifts to formal and material causes the history is far less recent, and consists in the biological and cultural forces that shaped a lump of meat into something that can run distance. Nevertheless, whether recent or distant, proximal or distal, the focus is on that which has, in the past, led up to the present. That the big-arsed-ape hypothesis has an air of parody provides an important clue to just how problematic these sorts of explanations can be.

The big-arsed-ape hypothesis emerged from a game my thoughts sometimes play with themselves – the 'I am built on something much older' game. But once you start playing that game, it's not clear why or when you should stop. When we came down from the trees, for example, it was as scavengers rather than hunters. So why think of myself as a big-arsed ape born to run any more than a shy, sly, scuttling eater of carrion left by animals that really were born to run. Before that, before we came down to earth, we were brachiators. Why should I consider myself a running ape over and above a brachiating one? Is it temporal proximity – I am closer in time to the running ape than the scavenging or brachiating ape? But if it is temporal proximity that is the key, then why am I not a couch-potato ape, an ape that has developed a keen, manipulative intelligence which it uses to get others to find its food – an ape whose large arse is really meant for sitting on? One day, I must play this 'I am built on something much older' game to its logical culmination and see where I end up.

Even if there is a way around this problem – even if there

is a legitimate reason for privileging the hunting ape in the constitution of what I am – there is another, more general problem. The 'I am built on something much older' game assumes that biological history can yield an unequivocal answer to the question of the sort of thing I am. But what if it yields no such thing? What if, instead, my biological history reveals me to be a confused melange of many different things, and the resulting whole only barely viable and coherent? Sometimes people have the idea that if evolution comes up with something – arses, legs, feet and so on – then whatever this is will be perfectly designed for the job at hand. This forgets that evolution is not so much life's architect as its handyman; a handyman of dubious competence and numerous mistakes who, in addition, finds himself working for a penny-pinching client. He can slap a bit of paint on here, slap a bit of paint on there. But he is never allowed to tamper significantly with the existing structure. That's the position evolution always finds itself in. The penny-pinching client is known as survival. You tamper too much with the existing structure – an extant creature – then survive is precisely what it is not going to do. The hurricane that is life is going to make short work of temporary scaffolding put in place while major structural changes are being made. The changes must always be small: gradual accretion of the minor is the game.

So, for example, evolution is presented with a fish. It used to swim happily in the ocean, but current vicissitudes of the environmental situation suggest that spending long periods of time lying camouflaged in the sand might be a good policy to adopt. So the fish lies on its side and gradually, for purposes of easy camouflaging, becomes flatter and flatter. What do you do about the eye, the one that lies buried in the mud all day? It is of no use where it is. And all things being equal – which, in the grand evolutionary scheme of things, they hardly ever are – it would be better if the fish had two eyes it could use to watch for predators and prey. So evolution has two options. The first: develop a new eye. But that will cost you. Lots of bodily and neural resources have to be put into that strategy. The second: deploy the unused eye that you've already got. Much cheaper. And so that is what evolution did. The grotesquely twisted features of the flatfish's face are testimony to its evolutionary history and to this parsimonious solution embodied in it. The eye that used to reside on the ventral side of a fish that swam for a living now twists around and relocates to what is now the dorsal side of a fish that spends most of its time in the sand. Evolution works like this. No one ever gives it a blank slate; it can only tinker with whatever is already there.

So we have to assume that there was an arboreal creature that, presumably due to the affordances or exigencies of environmental circumstance, began to spend more and more time on hazardous, but potentially profitable, terrestrial journeys. No one really knows why this was. Some speculate that the sorts of food offered by trees – leaves, sometimes fruit – no longer provided adequate sustenance. Others argue that we simply became too big for trees to offer us adequate protection from predators. The sorts of branches that could bear our weight would also support theirs. But, for whatever reason, a niche opened up that afforded opportunities for an ape willing to travel overland. At first living on the edge of riparian woodlands, our hominin ancestors gradually expanded their range. In this gradual expansion, those of our ancestors with bigger, more powerful legs – and what good are big legs without the big arse that powers them and provides ballast – survived at greater rates than those with weaker legs and smaller arses. And so the gene for a big arse multiplies and is passed down to us today.

But here is the snag. The big arse is still the point of connection between two essentially simian legs, on the ends of which are two essentially simian feet. Evolution is a handyman, not an architect. It has to work with what it is given. Admittedly, it has been working with the legs and feet too. They're now very different from those possessed by the ancestor we have in common with our simian cousins. But, nevertheless, evolution has to work with what it is given, and even then is not exactly perfect in its designs. We have to expect mistakes. There is no guarantee – far from it – that these simian legs and feet are going to be able to handle the stuff that this new turbocharged arse is going to get them to do. And if the simian legs and feet of some can handle it, there is no guarantee that this will be true of all of us, or even most.

In the end, the big-arsed-ape-that-was-born-to-run hypothesis is motivated by a kind of faith – a faith in evolution to have come up with a perfect solution to a cost-benefit problem presented to it by a tight-fisted client. That is a lot to ask of anything, especially a blind biological process. Over time, evolution does tend to get things more or less right. But this big-arsed-running-on-simian-legs-and-feet thing is just so new, comparatively speaking. It's not like hearts, lungs and blood. Evolution has had plenty of time to iron out the problems with those. These things take time, and I would be rather surprised if evolution has had enough time to comprehensively troubleshoot the problems with the strategy it used to produce humans. It may be that we are fractured creatures, even on the biological level. Were we born to run? From an appropriately distanced evolutionary perspective, we may have been born to do many things, not all of them, perhaps, entirely consistent. It may be that we are all mongrels, every living thing.

The fourth, and for Aristotle the most important, explanation of anything is its final cause: its why. The formal cause of something tells you what it is. The material cause tells you what it is made from. The efficient cause tells you what made or produced it. The remaining cause – what Aristotle called the final cause – tells you why it was made. The final cause of anything is its why. The final cause is the purpose of the activity, the reason why the activity is performed.

It may seem that I have already explained the final cause of running. I run to save my house and possessions from the jaws of one then two then three marauding canines. That certainly seems like the purpose of my run. My pack, and their destructive proclivities, provides the impetus for my running – they are its efficient cause. And then the purpose of the run is to mellow them out sufficiently to abstain from eating the few things I still actually possess. The final cause of my running is based on my desire to safeguard my remaining possessions. If I didn't care about these possessions – for example, if I didn't care whether or not Brenin chews holes in the sofa (happened), or whether Tess chews through the power cord of an almost new TV (happened, thankfully it wasn't plugged in at the time), and if I didn't care whether or not Nina chews a hole through a partition wall big enough for her to walk through (happened, though I'm not entirely sure there was enough evidence to pin it on Nina acting in isolation – she was simply the one caught red-handed), then the proclivities of the pack would provide no reason for me to run.

This, however, describes only the final cause of *my*

running, not the final cause of running itself. If this is the final cause of my running, others will have different final causes for their runs. After all, how many people run in order to persuade a pack of wolves and dogs to spare their possessions? Some people will run for the sake of their health, others to relieve the stresses of the office or perhaps even the family, others because they like the company it affords, and yet others because they like competing and accruing medals in the races they enter. And even when we restrict the focus to me, the particular final cause I cited will be operative only during a certain portion of my life. None of these reasons are the final cause of running – only of my running at a given time, your running at a given time, and so on.

As I pass Charles Fort, I turn left up a steep hill. This involves a couple of hundred yards of tough climb. I slog grimly onwards and upwards in the shadow of the Devil's Bastion. But this is nothing. I turn right, and head downhill again, past a farmhouse and some cottages, using the decline to stretch and loosen my muscles. I could have continued on up the hill, it would have soon levelled off, and I would have been left with a relatively easy mile or so home. On some days, if I am ill, I might take advantage of that. I continue on with the descent and at the bottom of the hill we turn left then right, and now I come to a grim but favourite part. I have been anticipating this since Charles Fort; the adrenalin started to course through me back then. We are at the foot of a hill that stretches away into the distance, and it is frighteningly steep; standing here at the bottom it looks more like a wall than a hill. My goal is to run up this hill, as fast as I possibly can. I must not stop, I must not falter: I must not even slow. If I do, the run has been a failure. It's an impossible goal – but sometimes they are the best.

I am looking straight down at my feet. If I raise my head, I feel like I will topple backwards. The hill starts off steep and then gets steeper. If I see any of this, if I see how far I have to go, if I see how long this pain will last, I know I will stop. My legs – driving, pumping – are on fire. My lungs feel as if they are turning themselves inside out trying to get the oxygen they need to combat the lactic burn. Keep going. Get to the next pothole, then the next. And then, finally: the hardest part of all. I'm reaching the top, the gradient is starting to level off: job done! No, the hard part is to keep going now, keep driving those legs as the lactic fire spreads outwards and is eventually replaced by a pervasive numb deadness; keep driving those legs as my lungs start to work again. Here is when the nausea kicks in, and it's worse than anything that has gone before. Sometimes – not often, but more than enough – I'll throw up; but I'll try to keep running as I do so. Finally, the nausea flooding my system is replaced with warm triumph. I roar, the pack bounces around me. And then, slowly, the gentle rhythm of the run takes over once more.

The days when this sort of endeavour might have actually had a point are long gone. I no longer play the sort of sports for which this torture might help. The most obvious facet of this ascent is its sheer pointlessness. I could jog up the hill; I could even walk – the pack wouldn't mind. But I charge up the hill. Here, although I did not understand it at the time, is a clue to the final cause of running – the real purpose not of my running, not of yours, but of running in general. It is not that there is a difference in kind between the charge up the hill and the rest of the run. It is just that in the charge up the hill the final cause of running is made particularly graphic. I was initially pushed into running by the jaws of one, then two, then three efficient causes. But the running I was pushed into has a final cause – a why – of its own.

On that hill, dying, gasping for breath, in mute lactic agony – at that precise moment in time, there was nothing in the world I would rather be doing. I ran that hill for one reason only: to run it. And that is a clue to the final cause of running. You and I may run for many reasons, but the purpose – the final cause – of running is always the same. At its best, and at its purest, the purpose of running is simply to run. Running is a member of the class of human activities that carry their purpose within themselves. The purpose of running is intrinsic to it. That, I would one day realize, is important.

4

American Dreams
2007

There is the whoosh of the cars on one side of us, and the slap and whir of the garden sprinklers on the other. Every run has its heartbeat. I am running with Nina and Tess through the early morning suburban streets of Miami. I left Alabama with Brenin twelve years ago. The intervening time has seen us run the green fields and plunging lanes of southern Ireland, the muddy woodlands of Wimbledon Common, the barren-as-boulders hills of the Pembrokeshire high country and then, finally, the sunset-golden beaches and fields of purple lavender – the way I shall always remember Languedoc. Brenin, my old friend, is gone now. His bones are buried in a sandy copse, beneath a ghost of stone that stands on the delta of the River Orb. After a long detour, for me at least, this is a return of sorts. A few days ago, we all moved to Miami. Poor old Nina and Tess, they have become old and they're not really capable of these runs any more. I've been in denial about this, but it ends here. Today is the last time I shall ever run with them. From now on, it will just be gentle walks. A little more than a year later they will both be dead. Tess went first, in the land of her father, victim of the same sort of cancer that claimed him. Nina went three weeks later, victim, I still think, of a broken heart.

This is the first run of my second life in the US. I cast my mind back to the last run of my first life here. That was a run of sadness: a run of times that had gone and would never come again. That was a run of fear: a run of times as yet unknown. I would soon, in a few short days, be putting Brenin on a plane to Ireland, and quarantine, but at that moment he floated along beside me as we ran through the early morning streets of Tuscaloosa. I was twenty-four when I moved there, fresh out of Oxford, and starting my first real job. I began Oxford-style. I went to work in blazer and flannels. I ended up grunge: T-shirt, shorts, flip-flops and a ponytail. I did not anticipate my first job turning into a seven-year party, but sometimes things have a funny way of turning out – it's one of life's most endearing features. After seven years, over a hundred rugby games, thousands of tequila shooters and more 25¢ longneck beers than I could number, I was ready to leave Alabama. When I had arrived there, I was younger than many of my students. So it was perhaps not particularly surprising that I had found my way into the university's student rugby team, and the rather surreal subculture that surrounded it. But before I knew it I was thirty-one. I was too old, and the party had moved on. There is only so long you can turn up at student parties – even student rugby parties – without it getting first a little sad and then a little creepy. I suspected I had already transgressed the borders of sad, and wanted to get the hell out of Dodge before I crossed over into creepy. No one comes back from creepy.

American Dreams

Brenin had been my constant companion for my last four years in Alabama. For four years, every bar, every party, every road trip, Brenin had been there with me, mute and impartial witness to the beers and the chasers and shooters – to the women I had chased and the women who had chased me. I was going to detach myself from what was becoming, with quiet inevitability, the wreckage of a life. We were moving to Ireland, somewhere quiet where I could write. But Brenin had first to go into quarantine, and I would not see my friend and brother for the next six months.

It was an early Sunday morning. We'd had a game the previous day, followed by the inevitable festivities and so I was running off the party of the night before. My memories of those streets are pallid. In this respect they are not inaccurate, for the streets were also pallid. Once the blinding-white porched-and-pillared abodes of respectable southern gentility, that part of town had been taken over by the students of the University of Alabama, and the houses were grey and cracked and peeling from all the young lives that had burned brightly within them. But my memories are pallid and peeling for another reason. They were made in a time when I had little need for them. Age is not, in fact, the destroyer of memories; that belongs to youth. Age is the preserver of memories, the reverer of memories. The memories I make become stronger as I get older. The memories I made in my youth are sickly children.

I knew the people who lay dreaming in those shattered houses that lined the streets. I had taught some of them, played rugby with some of them and been to parties with many of them. I knew the people and I knew their dreams, at least the dreams they were willing to tell. Most of them were dreams by proxy – dreams their parents dreamed, that grew inside of them apace with the yet-to-be-born child. These were dreams of doctors and lawyers: dreams of big money and big houses, of expensive cars and attractive spouses. This was America, where you could be whatever you want to be if you were prepared to work hard enough. This was the great dream. This was the great lie. Most of these dreams would fail my sleeping friends. By the time I returned to America, they would have found newer, smaller dreams.

This first run of my second life in America is not taking place in real Miami. By that I mean it is not the sort of thing you would think about when you think about Miami, not if you live somewhere else. When someone who is not from Miami thinks of Miami, they probably think of South Beach, or Downtown: the sort of skyscapes and art-deco-ed ocean front they would cut to on *CSI: Miami*, just to let you know you're watching *CSI: Miami* and not *CSI: NY*. But we could be anywhere – at least, anywhere the streets are lined with palm and banyan trees. In fact, we are in Palmetto Bay, a decidedly bourgeois suburb about ten miles south of the centre of Miami, or where the centre of Miami would probably be if it actually had a centre. Horatio Caine wouldn't be seen dead in Palmetto Bay – nothing ever happens here. Our presence in this place is a sign of how things are changing. Nina and Tess may be fading, but there is new life on the way. Emma, my wife, is four months pregnant, and we're living the safe, solid, respectable life of a safe, solid, respectable middle-class couple. I have school zones to think about now – or, rather, Emma does; it would never have occurred to me – and Palmetto Bay has the best state schools in Miami-Dade.

Twenty minutes into this debut run, I have already decided I hate running in Miami. It's not the heat or humidity. This is

January, it's a bright, pleasant early morning and I would guess the temperature to be in the high sixties – it will climb to the upper seventies by the afternoon – and humidity won't become an inconvenience for a few more months. By the time that happens, I'll look back with fondness on these winter runs. It's the flatness of it all that I hate; the unremitting monotony of these suburban death flats. There's nothing to break up the run: nothing to grimly prepare for when approaching the bottom, or breathlessly exult in when reaching the top.

When you come from Wales and now live in Miami, you tend to miss the mountains. You don't necessarily miss much else, but you do miss the mountains – or hills, or any sort of gradient really. Some areas of Miami have 'heights' in their name – Richmond Heights, Olympia Heights. It's a sick joke. They're eight feet above sea level – nosebleed country in these parts. Sometimes I'll find myself staring fondly at the Rickenbacker Causeway, the biggest gradient in Miami-Dade County. At weekends, if you drive over the causeway to Key Biscayne, you'll see scores of cyclists going back and forth over it. The causeway is arched and it's the largest 'hill' they have to practise on.

Perhaps the cyclists find their avocation as frustrating here as I find running. But I think for me it's even worse. At least they actually get somewhere. I haven't yet discovered what I will come to call, for entirely obvious reasons, 'snakeland' – the strip of land off Old Cutler Road, where, in years to come, I will run with a dog that is yet to be born. For now, it's the suburbs and we are getting, precisely, nowhere. Things are so spread-out in this country; the cities are extended, they were built around the car – something I had forgotten during my European hiatus. We started at the house on 146th Street, and we ran north up 77th Avenue, towards 136th Street. There we turned east, and are now approaching Old Cutler Road. If we turn south down Old Cutler to 152nd, and then west to 77th and back to the house, that will be pretty much five miles; and that's certainly as much as Nina and Tess can handle now. There's a brief flirtation with the border of Pinecrest, but we won't even have left Palmetto Bay. And accompanying us for every stride is the whoosh of the cars and the slap and whir of the sprinklers on carefully manicured lawns.

It is 6.30 a.m., and the rush hour has already started. Everyone takes 77th at this time of the day because US 1 – or 'Useless 1' as they call it here – will be gridlocked. I think many Miamians would shower in their cars if they could: Starbucks for coffee and muffins to go, eating and drinking, combing and brushing, texting and honking their way to the day's business. And while Lake Okeechobee, which supplies the water to Miami, is at a record low, the garden sprinklers are spinning, spitting plumes of water as far as the eye can see. All around me people rush to work so they can make money to pay gardeners to cut their grass that grows so fast because of the whir and the slap of their sprinklers.

Americans have fewer holidays than anyone else in the developed world. There is no federally mandated requirement for paid vacation time at all. And while there are ten public holidays, many Americans work through them. In contrast, in France, our previous country of residence, they have a little more *savoir faire*, at least in the art of living: the French are guaranteed thirty days of paid vacation every year, on top of their ten public holidays. Brazilians also do this right: thirty days' mandatory paid vacation plus eleven public holidays. Lithuania, Finland, Russia – their citizens can all expect forty days or more of paid vacation and public holidays a year. Americans work. They are anxious, and not without reason. If the loss of a job, and therefore health insurance, should coincide with a serious (or even not so serious) illness, they will become bankrupt.

But the anxiety is more pervasive than that. This is a country built on consumption. For many, basic needs are easily met and so consumption quickly turns into the buying of things you don't need. These things will quickly break, I suspect largely because they have been designed to do so. To convince someone to buy something they do not need is not difficult: you simply make them afraid of the consequences of not buying it. Fear is the great friend of consumption. The things I now have to worry about at night, instead of sleeping (which Americans also seem to worry about a lot): yellow grass (if you have it, you will be shunned by your neighbours), crabgrass (even worse than yellow grass, consider yourself doubly shunned), termites (can apparently raze your house to the ground in seconds), bees (mostly Africanized down here, you know), queen palm disease (it's going around), hurricanes (self-evident), coconuts (the number-three cause of non-vehicular-related accidental death in South Florida, after pools and lightning; and anyway, hurricanes can turn them into lethal projectiles). And this list has been compiled purely from business cards left in my mailbox in the few days since we arrived.

If you listen carefully, in the whooshing, hissing, slapping and whirring of the sprinklers you will hear the American Dream.

Moritz Schlick was a well-known German philosopher of the 1920s and 1930s, one of the founding members of the so-called Vienna Circle, a group of philosophers of science who became known as the logical positivists. He was shot and killed by a deranged student on the campus of the University of Vienna in 1936. I have been thinking about teaching a course on the meaning of life, and recently stumbled upon a paper Schlick wrote. It is entitled 'On the Meaning of Life' and Schlick wrote this when he was a young man, before he became a famous positivist. It is a gem of a paper, very unpositivist, not at all the sort of thing you would normally associate with Schlick. 'I do not know whether the burden of purpose has ever weighed more heavily on mankind than at the present time. The present idolizes work.' He wrote that in 1927. And, as far as I am aware, he never even saw America. We turn south down Old Cutler Road. Whoosh, slap, whir, whoosh, slap, whir: all around me pulses the American Dream. Moritz Schlick understood that it was idolatry.

Most of the things I do in my life I do for the sake of something else. The purpose of my activity is rarely found in the activity itself, but only in something else that the activity allows me to get. But this means that the value of the activity is also not to be found in the activity itself, but only in this other thing that the activity affords me. If I run simply for health, or because it helps me stay alive, and if this is the only purpose of my running, then the value of the run lies in the health it promotes, in the life it prolongs. It is true, of course, that health and a long life are valuable things. I would not want to deny something as obvious as this. My point concerns the relation between the value of running and the value of things like this. If I run only for the sake of things like health or a long life, running's value consists only in these other things that it allows me to get. In itself, running would have no value. If the purpose of an activity is not to be found in the activity, neither is the value of that activity.

As I mentioned in the foreword, things I do only for the sake of something else have what philosophers call 'instrumental' value – their value is as an instrument that allows me to get this something else. In contrast, an activity is intrinsically valuable if it has value in itself, independently of anything else it might allow me to get. It is not immediately obvious that there is anything I do that is valuable in itself. But I had better hope there is something: if there is not, then as Aristotle pointed out, nothing in my life has value. Suppose A is valuable only because of B, and B is valuable only because of C, and so on. There are two basic possibilities. First, as I continue the series, I eventually encounter something – call it Z – that has intrinsic value: something that is valuable in itself and not merely for the sake of something else. In this case, the value of everything leading up to Z derives from the intrinsic value of Z: this value grounds the instrumental value of everything else. The other possibility is that there is no Z: I never manage to find anything that has intrinsic value. Then there would be nothing that could ground the instrumental value of anything else. The value of everything in my life would always be deferred – always just out of reach. My life would resemble the punishment of Tantalus, standing in a pool of water beneath a tree laden with fruit. Whenever Tantalus reaches for the fruit, the tree's branches raise themselves out of his reach. Whenever he stoops to drink, the water recedes before he can get to it. A life that has no intrinsic value in it is, in this sense, 'tantalizing'.

When I do something only for the sake of something else, what I am doing is, Schlick argued, a form of work. This is somewhat broader than its usual sense and would include things not ordinarily thought of as work. However, work, in its usual sense, is a classic example of work in this broader sense. I work because I want to be paid. The payment is the external goal – the for-the-sake-of-which – towards which my work is directed. Similarly, if I run only because I want to stay healthy, or because I want to stay alive, then my running is work: an activity that is directed towards something outside it, something that gives it its purpose and value. If I run because I think that Nina and Tess need or enjoy it, my running is also work – in this case work aimed at benefiting someone else rather than me.

Instrumentally valuable activity is work. Therefore, intrinsically valuable activity is, as Schlick also concluded, a form of play. The value of work always lies in something else – something that is not work. In itself, work has no value. The expression 'instrumental value' is, to this extent, unfortunate and misleading. It suggests that work has value, but this is merely of a specific sort – instrumental. In fact, to say that something has instrumental value is to say that its value always lies in something else – and so it is in this something else that the value is really found. That is, if something has merely instrumental value then it has, itself, no value at all. Play, on the other hand, is quite different. It has intrinsic value: it is something done for its own sake and therefore, by definition, has value in itself. Play has value, but work does not. It obviously follows that play must be more valuable than work. As Schlick put it: 'The great gospel of our industrial age has been exposed as idolatry. The greater part of our existence, filled as it is with goal-seeking work at the behest of others, has no value in itself, but obtains this only by reference to the festive hours of play, for which work provides merely the means and the preconditions.' A life of work is redeemed only through play. When we play, we do not chase value – for the value of play does not lie outside itself – we are immersed in it.

I may not be enjoying today's run – in fact, I am pretty sure it is work and not play – but I am enjoying the irony of this conclusion. I have just returned to the land that is – supposedly – built on the rejection of play. The rejection of communism in favour of capitalism is just a symptom of something deeper. America is the nation that rejected play in favour of work – or, at least, that's a common foundation myth that some of its citizens like to promulgate. We are put here, on this earth, to work hard. Work is inherently ennobling. Play is frivolous. I feel deliciously subversive: an outsider in a much deeper way than a mere communist ever could be.

Perhaps it is the utter lack of a gradient that causes me to cast my thoughts back fondly to the hill I used to run in Kinsale: the near-vertical wall I would charge up as fast as I possibly could. Whatever the reason, this is where my thoughts find themselves and, for the first time, I think I understand exactly what I was doing on that hill and why I was doing it. I was playing a game with the hill.

The twentieth-century Austrian philosopher Ludwig Wittgenstein claimed that the word 'game' cannot be defined. A definition would have to specify a common feature shared by all games and only games, and there is no such feature. Games need have nothing in common with each other. What unites them is mere family resemblance. A father might share a nose with his son, but not his eyes. These eyes may be shared with the mother, who lacks the nose. The chin may be shared with an uncle, or sibling, but not with either of the parents. The family has a 'look'; but this is not grounded in any common feature that all its members share. Games, Wittgenstein claimed, are like this. Instead of a common feature, there is a series of overlapping similarities. This network of similarity is what allows us to regard activities as games. This model, Wittgenstein argued, provided a useful way of thinking about concepts in general, not just the concept of a game.

Wittgenstein is, not without justification, one of the most famous philosophers of the twentieth century. Perhaps for this reason, most philosophers seem to think he is right about games and concepts more generally. Comparatively few, outside the small community of philosophers of sport, have heard of Bernard Suits – a Canadian philosopher who died a few years ago. However, Suits did what Wittgenstein said could not be done: came up with a perfectly adequate definition of the word 'game'. That is, he identified a common feature that all games share – a feature that makes them all games. According to Suits, a game is an activity in which we voluntarily choose an inefficient means of achieving a goal, and we do this just so we can engage in the activity. Put in Suitsist terms, my entanglements with the hill can be analysed as follows. First, there is what he calls the 'pre-lusory' goal. This is a goal that can be specified independently of the game. The pre-lusory goal is to get from the bottom of the hill to the top of the hill. This goal has nothing essentially to do with running. I can get from the bottom to the top of the hill in various ways. An easy way would be to drive up there. A gentle stroll would also be far easier than running full-tilt. What I bring to this pre-lusory goal is what Suits called a 'lusory attitude'. (from the Latin *ludus*, meaning game). I want to achieve the pre-lusory goal, but not just in any way. I want to achieve it in a peculiarly difficult way: by running as fast as I can. It is this lusory attitude that makes my achieving the pre-lusory goal a game. When we play a game we, in essence, make things difficult for ourselves. We choose a difficult way of doing something – something that could be done more easily – and we do this precisely so we can play the game. I am, therefore, playing a game with the hill (in the sense that one plays tennis with a racquet, rather than that in which one plays tennis with an opponent).

The same is true of running in general, and not just the running of that particularly intransigent hill. In running, the goal is to get from A to B – or to get from being at A at a given time to also being at A at a later time, if you begin and end at your own house – and there are various ways of achieving this pre-lusory goal: driving, walking, cycling. Indeed, if the goal is to get from A to A, then all you need to do is stay put. To run is to voluntarily choose a relatively difficult way of achieving this pre-lusory goal. This is true of games in general, not just running games: to play a game is to adopt a (relatively) difficult way of achieving a goal that could, in principle, always be achieved by other, less difficult, means. We do this precisely so we can engage in the activity of achieving the goal in this way: we do it precisely so we can play the game. All running can be play – it depends on why one does it. In fact, it seems I must go further than this. The essence of running is play – play is what running essentially is – and even when one runs for other, specific, reasons, play keeps continually reasserting itself at the heart of running. Running may be hard, but when it is done properly it is not hard work. Play can be hard too – as hard as any work. I have always presented my running, both to other people and to myself, as a response to the pressure exerted on me by three large and destructive canines. I believed this and at one time it might even have been true. But now I'm beginning to understand that it can only be part of the truth. Those animals needed to be kept as exhausted as possible – that is true. But I could have chosen easier ways of doing it. I could have walked the fields rather than run the lanes – the dogs would have run almost as much, or even more if the fields were full of rabbits. I could have used my mountain bike regularly – and not just when I was injured. When I chose to run with them, and when I continued to run with them day in day out, I was choosing to play. And now, courtesy of Moritz Schlick and Bernard Suits, I am beginning to see why I chose this. To run, indeed to play any game, is to be in direct contact – as direct a contact as is possible – with intrinsic value in life.

Running, however, is a particularly pure example of contact with intrinsic value because it is what we might call an 'undifferentiated' activity – a peculiarly undifferentiated game. It is unstructured, or far less structured than most other forms of play. At the other end of the athletic spectrum, we find sports like cricket and tennis that are highly differentiated in the sense that they are broken down into discrete parts. The game of cricket is broken down into innings, which are broken down into overs, which are broken down into individual deliveries. Tennis is, similarly, segmented into sets that are broken down into games that are, in turn, broken down into individual points. In these sports, the advice is to play each ball or point as it comes, and there is a familiar phenomenon – known as 'choking' or 'the yips' – which results from a failure to heed this advice. You choke when your focus switches from the individual point you are playing or delivery you are facing and start worrying about your situation in the wider context of the game – or, indeed, how you fared on previous points or even in previous games. If you think your place in the cricket team is under threat because you have not been scoring many runs lately, you may well get the yips. If you think this point in a tennis game you are playing is crucial because if you lose it you also lose the set, you may well choke. The antidote to choking or the yips is always the same: focus on this moment, this point, this delivery and nothing else.

We can understand this phenomenon in terms of the ideas of intrinsic and instrumental value. In focusing on the individual point and nothing else, one comes to see that point as being valuable for what it is in itself. As soon as this focus is lost, the individual point comes to have only instrumental value – its value becomes tied to its place or role in the wider game. The point becomes important because of what it means or signifies, and not because of what it is. Once this happens, you are lost: you choke. When you play each point as it comes, or play each delivery on its own merits, you are doing just that: playing. But when the value of each point or delivery becomes instrumental, what you are doing is work.

A run is not differentiated or structured like this. It has no discernible parts. There are individual strides and swingings of arms, but these all flow into each other. So a run, in effect, has the same status as an individual segment in a highly structured game. At its best, it is something done for its own sake, play not work. Even when it is done for other reasons, its essential nature as play has a way of reasserting itself.

We live in a narrowly instrumental age, and the idea of something that is done for its own sake is one received only with great difficulty. Nothing can be done for its own sake – everything must be done for the sake of something else. Even games, we assume, must have some instrumental purpose. When animals play, we are told, they do so in order to acquire skills – predatory, evasive – that will be useful in later life. The same is true of children – their play is an important part in the overall process whereby they become 'socialized'. The message is in each case the same: play is not really play – it is work. I do not want to deny of course that what seems like play can really be work. Conversely, many things that seem like work can really be play. The difference between work and play does not lie in what you do, but why you do it. As Schlick put it: 'Human action is work, not because it bears fruit, but only when it proceeds from, and is governed by, the thought of its fruit.' By the same token, action is play when it is done simply in order to do it. Whether or not the action has other beneficial consequences is irrelevant to whether it counts as play. So even if it is true that the function of play is to somehow equip you for later life, play is still play as long as you do what you do for no other reason than that you want to.

Does this idea of playing for the sake of playing even make sense? If I run because I want to run, then surely that is because I enjoy it. But then the enjoyment, the pleasure that running gives me, would seem to be the external goal of the run. And so, it seems, my running counts as work after all. But this inference would be premature. The enjoyment of running is part of what it is to run. There is no such thing as enjoyment in the abstract. There is only this or that form of enjoyment. Compare the enjoyment of running with the enjoyment of chess; the enjoyment of sex with the enjoyment of winning. There is no general type of thing – enjoyment in general, non-specific enjoyment – that all these things share. There is simply the enjoyment of running, the enjoyment of chess, the enjoyment of sex and the enjoyment of winning. Running is not simply a physical activity – the putting of one foot in front of another until a certain distance has been covered. It is also a mental activity. The enjoyment of running is not an external goal towards which running is aimed. It is an integral part of the activity of running.

This is hidden by the word 'enjoyment' – a peculiarly unhelpful and disingenuous word. Often, enjoyment is thought of as a pleasant feeling. Since the same feeling can, in principle, be produced in different ways – a suitably designed pill, for example, might be able to induce the requisite feelings of pleasure – this might lead one to think that the enjoyment of running is extrinsic to it. If this is what enjoyment is – pleasant feelings – then I suspect enjoyment is only tangentially connected to running: the mental life of running cannot be captured in this way. I have tried to capture the essence of this mental life in terms of the idea of the heartbeat of the run – the place of dancing thoughts. There is no pill that can take you to this place. The heartbeat of the run is intrinsic to the run. It is perhaps true that I run to become lost in the heartbeat of the run. But this is just another way of saying I run for the sake of running.

In this respect – the peripheral character of enjoyment – running and writing are kindred activities. Writing is not a game: there is no pre-lusory goal toward which I bring to bear a lusory attitude. But, as Suits also points out, not all playing is the playing of a game. Writing can be play; and it can also be work. It all depends on why I do it. If I am writing something only because I have to – I have entered into some contractual agreement, for example – then my writing

95

is work. But my best writing is never like this. My best writing happens when I simply find all these ideas flying around in my head, and I do not know exactly what they are or where they lead, but feel compelled to find out. I write because I want to know what it is I am thinking, and I never really know this until I see it on the page in front of me. I trap ideas in the form of words, inspect and assess them. This play has a value all of its own and, when I engage in it, there is nothing in the world I would rather be doing. To write is to play with shiny, sparkly, twinkling ideas. When writing becomes work – these ideas become muted and stale. But little, if any, of this has to do with enjoyment in the traditional sense. Often it is more like torture – more like running that hill of Kinsale.

Running that hill was a game of a special sort – and it is easy to see how little this game had to do with enjoyment in the conventional sense. The game involved intense suffering, not pleasure; nor was this torture redeemed by the dancing thoughts of the run's heartbeat. This was a game of enduring, of finding out how much would break me. I always ran that hill just to see if I could – to see if I could still make myself do it today just as I had done it yesterday. Finding out if the hill would beat me – knowing one way or the other – that was the point of this game within a game; it was a game of knowing. Sometimes knowing, of this sort at least, is also part of what it is run.

I started my life of running as an adult with instrumental goals in mind. And on any given day, I can run with instrumental goals in mind. But once I reach the run's heartbeat, the place of dancing thoughts, these goals have long been left behind. Once again, I have Schlick to thank for helping me understand why. He wrote: 'It is the joy in sheer creation,

the dedication to the activity, the absorption in the movement, which transforms work into play. As we know there is
a great enchantment which almost always brings this transformation about – rhythm. To be sure, it will only work
perfectly where it is not brought externally and deliberately
to the activity, and artificially coupled with it, but evolves
spontaneously from the nature of the action and its natural
form.' Once the rhythm of the run has done its hypnotic
work, when the heartbeat of the run emerges 'spontaneously
from the nature of the action and its natural form', I am running only to run. Before that, I am not running, not really: I
am simply moving. This point when motion transforms into
running – this is the point when work becomes play. My
body moves, but my thoughts play in the place my mind
used to be.

If running is intrinsically valuable, then the heartbeat of the
run, it would seem, is its experiential correlate. To experience the heartbeat of the run is to experience intrinsic value.
The heartbeat of the run is intrinsic value making itself
known in the world: it is something that is important in life
revealing itself to me.

Some people have at least flirted with the idea that running
is something like a religion, or with the idea that the experience of running is something like a religious experience. But
I think the heartbeat of the run is actually the antithesis of
religion or, at least, of one way of thinking about religion.
The way of thinking about religion I have in mind is exem-
plified by Tolstoy. I remember reading, many years ago,
Tolstoy's 'My Confession': an honest, moving, if perhaps a
little melodramatic, account of the way Tolstoy came to think
of the meaning of life. When he had reached a certain point in

his life, Tolstoy became afflicted with questions of a certain form: 'So what?' 'And then?' 'Why?' I have six thousand *desyatinas* of land in Samara and three hundred horses. So what? Moreover, I'm going to be more famous than Gogol, Pushkin, Shakespeare and Molière. And then? Consequently, I am able to provide a good education and a comfortable life for my children. Why? Tolstoy's inability to answer these questions upset him – a lot. 'If I did not answer them, I could not live.'

He explains this *prise de conscience* with an allegory. A traveller in an Eastern land jumps into a well to escape the attentions of an 'infuriated beast'. However, at the bottom of the well is a dragon. Caught between beast and dragon, the traveller finds himself clinging to a branch of a small bush that grows out of a cleft in the wall. Then, just when he thinks that things cannot get any worse, they inevitably do. Two mice, one black, one white, appear and start nibbling on the branch. At any moment, the branch is going to break and the traveller will fall to his death. He knows this. Nevertheless, while he is still hanging there, he sees some drops of honey hanging on the leaves of the bush. The traveller reaches out for the honey with his tongue and licks the leaves. Similarly, Tolstoy thought, he clings grimly to the branch of life, knowing that the dragon of death is waiting for him. He tries to lick the honey, which used to give him pleasure but no longer does. And the white and black mice of day and night nibble away at the life to which he is clinging. This is not a fable, Tolstoy claimed: it is 'veritable, indisputable, comprehensible truth'.

The 'truth' in question seems to be a certain sort of realization coupled with a series of inferences based on that knowledge. At least part of Tolstoy's realization is that he is going to die – not just as an abstract possibility that will eventually catch up with him somewhere down the line, but as a concrete reality, understood viscerally rather than intellectually. The result: the honey is no longer sweet. Nothing matters. It is not just his death that disturbs him. Sooner or later, he cheerfully continues, my family will become ill, suffer and die, and there will be nothing left but 'stench and worms'. Also, there is the question of his work – his non-biological legacy. In the blink of an eye, he realizes, it will all be forgotten.

Medieval philosophers had an expression: *sub specie aeternitatis* – under the gaze of eternity. Actually, you do not need eternity, any sufficiently long-term view will do. Under the gaze of eternity or, at any rate, a sufficiently long time, any trace that Tolstoy ever existed will be erased. He will have disappeared, so will everyone he ever loved, and his work will beat a rapid path after him into the long good night. In terms of his artistic legacy – he has done better than most of us. One hundred years after his death his work is still widely read and highly regarded. But even so, a few more hundred years and who knows? A few thousand years and the odds lengthen considerably. Even if his works last as long as the human race, this is but the blink of an eye in the cosmic scheme of things. Disappearance waits for all of us, even Tolstoy. The ancient Greeks had an idea of what they called 'objective immortality' – the survival of a person through their work. But, unfortunately, objective procrastination would be a more accurate label. It is just putting off the inevitable. So what? And then? Why?

Tolstoy's reaction to this was a familiar one: he sought solace in faith, faith in the promise of a life after this one. Faith is what connects we who do not last long with the infinite and eternal. 'No matter what answers faith may give, its every answer gives to the finite existence of man the sense of the infinite – a sense which is not destroyed by suffering, privation and death. Consequently, in faith alone could we find the meaning and possibility of life.'

This is one expression of the religious view of life. I do not mean to suggest it is the only view of life licensed by religion, but it is certainly a common one. According to this view, the value of this life is to be found in the next life – as long as we go to the right place. So this life has merely instrumental value. It is valuable to the extent that it prepares us for, and provides us entry to, the life that is to come. In the heartbeat of the run, I think I experience the antithesis of this attitude. I experience intrinsic value in this life. The experience is, therefore, an affirmation that there are things we do in this life that are intrinsically valuable.

Tolstoy, I think, is right to this extent. Any satisfying account of the meaning of life must be capable of redeeming life. Life is horrific in ways that Tolstoy identified, and also, I think, in ways that he did not. Running may point to intrinsic value in this life. But a meaning to life would require more than intrinsic value in life. It would require that this intrinsic value be important enough, big enough, to balance – in our dreams, perhaps even outweigh – the horror of life. Can what is valuable for its own sake and not for the sake of anything else do this? Can I infer meaning in life from value in life? I am not sure. To do that, I must think more about the horror of life. I must reduce it to its most basic principles. I must identify its essence.

We are in the home stretch, Nina and Tess still cling grimly to my heels and I give them each a little pat of encouragement. 'Nearly home now, a big drink of water for you when we get there' – that always gives them a little boost. The ears prick up and they press on with new enthusiasm. We run beside the royal palms that line this part of 77th Avenue. This really is a world away, and for Nina and Tess it is a lifetime away, from the hedgerowed lanes of Kinsale when they were still young dogs and charged up that hill with me day in and day out. Over the canal bridge we go and in through the gates of the community. When we reach the bottom of the driveway, I stop at the mailbox. Someone has left a business card there, someone who apparently pressure-cleans roofs. On the back is scrawled a terrifying handwritten message: 'Roof mold eats tiles – call us.' Ah yes, fear – the greatest friend of the tyranny of purpose. Back to work.

5

The Serpent of Eden
2009

Scrub oaks, gnarled and twisted, scowl down on either side of the narrow path; a path clogged with rotting leaves and the fallen fronds of royal palms. In the tropics, there is no winter: the leaves fall from the trees in the spring but are quickly replaced. In Miami, it is early morning in early May and already there is the heat. It scours the forest for the last hiding places of the night's steamy cool, searching under stones, digging down into the fissures where the rattlers live. Its moist and persistent fingers reach into my mouth, my nostrils; slithering their way into my lungs, insinuating themselves into my blood, thin and quick.

The path beneath me is old coral, shattered and withered, laced with the roots of trees, the jungle's hardened arteries that knot the path together, binding and penetrating the coral. Every twisted root looks like a snake; every new step is a leap of faith. A tropical forest is life in fast-forward. Here, we live fast, die young. This is a forest gorged on life, choked with life, and the hot, wet stench of decay that clings to everything is the mocking response of time, laughing at life's impatient futility. The forest knows lives as Rimbaud knew lives. They are the *worms that crawl on a banner of meat that bleeds, under a sea of silken flowers.*

In Tuscaloosa, the heartbeat of the run was a solid thump-thump into the softened summer tarmac. In Ireland, on the Rathmore Peninsula of Kinsale, the heartbeat was thud-shh-shh-thud-shh-shh, as my steps quickly faded into the enveloping wind. In suburban Miami, it is the whoosh of the cars and the slap and whir of the garden sprinklers. But here in jungle Miami, the beat is utterly distinctive: thud-rustle-pitter-pat-thud-rustle-pitter-pat. Every time my foot hits the ground, an anole – a diminutive but ubiquitous indigenous lizard – scurries away into the deeper undergrowth, its tiny feet tap-tapping on the leaves. You quickly learn the frequency of the anole on the leaves. When the frequency diminishes – a longer rustle, no pitter-pat – then you stop. You stop dead, because that is a snake.

Hugo is a German shepherd, and on the day of this run he is a little over eighteen months old. On the following page, he is pictured in the garden of our Miami home. The picture was taken earlier this year, just after we had returned from one of our morning runs. He is now requesting that I throw his Frisbee, a laconic canine comment on the feeble four-mile run I was able to offer him. Is that the best you've got, old man? Of course, this picture was taken back in the Miami winter. At this time, he had only just matured enough to run regularly, and he hadn't yet had the pleasure of footing it in a Miami summer. Talk to me again after that, son.

Hugo is tall for a German shepherd, around thirty inches at

the shoulder, and lean – weighing about eighty pounds. He'll fill out to around ninety when he is fully grown; no more than that I think. His feet are still a little too big for him, which adds a certain ungainly charm to his movements, especially when he switches from canter to sprint. He is dark – his body black, except for the red of his chest, underbelly, legs and feet. Hugo is from Germany – a foreigner like me.

Not only outsiders, we are minor outlaws. Our little runs are in defiance of the law. Miami is the most dog-unfriendly place I have ever heard of, let alone lived in; although, from what I gather, everywhere is becoming dog-unfriendly (part of a more general unfriendliness, I suspect). One's every turn is dogged – no pun intended – with a draconian set of laws that require dogs to be leashed in all public places. Except, of course, in the specially designated dog parks – I think there are three in the entire city, tiny faeces-strewn enclosures, where one can barely swing a cat let alone walk a dog. And anyway Hugo needs to run, not walk. And at his pace, not mine – not tied to me like a prisoner. If he can't run, his soul will die. And so we find ourselves running where we can't be seen.

I have grown old and young again many times. When the pack that runs beside me grows old and can no longer run with me, I stay at home and grow old with them. Today I am becoming young again, although that is not how it feels. Growing young again is hard work – harder every time. Once I get my youth back, running will once again be a treat for both body and soul. Today, that's only half true. If I can keep going long enough for the pain in my knee to subside; if my back doesn't seize up, or my calf give out on me; if I can just put up with the pain in my Achilles for the first mile or two, it will usually fade after that; if I can just get enough air into these ageing lungs, get this ancient and cloudy blood gushing through stiffening arteries – then maybe once again my body can have a little party on the endorphins. But that's unlikely on today's run with Hugo in snakeland. I have only recently started running again with Hugo, after a long, long lay-off.

This lay-off was the result of two things. When we first moved to Miami, I tried running with Nina and Tess – just once, because it was clear they couldn't do it any more. So they stopped running and consequently I stopped running. It was the guilt: I couldn't deal with the reproachful looks every time I tried to leave the house in running gear. Why aren't you taking us? What have we done? Tess passed away in February of last year. She was ten years old. Nina was twelve when this happened and a very old, very frail dog. I really didn't see just how old and frail. Nina hung on for three weeks after Tess died, rattling around the house looking for her old friend, and then suffered massive organ failure. I'd just returned from a speaking engagement in the Netherlands – a long-standing commitment I couldn't get out of – and I'd been away for three days. Emma told me that Nina was a little off-colour, but I put it down to my absence coming so soon after Tess's disappearance. My diagnosis was apparently confirmed when she perked up on my late-night arrival, and we split a small pizza. The next morning when we came downstairs, she couldn't stand. I carried her into the vet, just as I had done for Tess three weeks earlier. It was awful for us that they went so close together, but without any doubt the best for them. And I'm happy it turned out that way.

After a while, we acquired Hugo as a tumbling eight-week-old puppy – a first-birthday present for our son, Brenin, was the spin I put on it. And, it is true, Brenin had known Nina and Tess since he was two days old – his first word was 'dog' – and he missed them when they went. That was around a year ago – you should not run with a big dog until he's at least a year old; his growing bones are just not ready for it. Putting together the absence of a dog that needs to run and the night-after-night of sleep deprivation that goes hand in hand with a restless and demanding baby boy, I just could not manage to persuade myself to run. At least, not regularly – and if I don't do it regularly, running becomes a deeply unpleasant slog: work not play. And so I stopped running completely.

So it has been a long time – two years all told – and this is the first time I've got back to running regularly since we moved to Miami and since I became a father. I have become a fat and slow father. With the run of today, I'm slowly working my way back and the former experiential perquisites of the run just haven't started happening for me yet. When I am in better shape, and the rhythm of the run holds me in its spell, my thoughts will dance in a way they never seem to do when I am not running. But that will not happen today. The thoughts that come today are slower, languid, like the gentle rustle of snakes in the undergrowth. These are thoughts that come from exhaustion without rhythm. Perhaps these are thoughts that would not appear – thoughts my brain would not allow – when I am in a less weakened state. Meditation through mortification of the body: an ancient tradition that lives on in this little part of south Florida where Hugo and I run today.

I hope Hugo enjoys these runs. I think he does. His young life is certainly impatient enough to be on the road in the mornings. But perhaps he understands that the longer I dally at my computer, recording and inspecting whatever ideas the night has offered up, the more the growing heat will make us suffer. Perhaps he wants to be out and safely back home to the swimming pool before the snakes come out for their midday bask on the paths and boulders of coral that a younger sea has sprinkled through the forest. If so, I share these sentiments.

Hugo presses on. When we are in the woods, he must run behind me. The woods are alive with snakes. If I'm bitten, it's going to smart, but ultimately I'll be okay, probably. If he's bitten, then the prognosis is less clear. A bite to the legs or snout – he'll probably survive. A bite to the torso – his chances are not so good. But he is young and impatient, and he wants to see what life has in store for him further up the trail. He presses at my heels, nearly tripping me up. 'Back!' I snarl, gesticulating with my thumb, but smiling inwardly at this echo of years gone by. He dutifully drops a few paces back, a resolution that he will soon forget.

For obvious reasons, I'm teaching Hugo to fear the snake. It's not hard: I fear the snake. And one thing we parents are very good at is transferring our fears to our children. I'm not as bad as Emma. She has a general-purpose, context-independent, turned-to-stone terror of snakes. You merely have to say the word 'snake' and she blanches. Once, a number of years ago on our first holiday together, we were eating at the Hard Rock Cafe in Key West, and a man – a street performer – appeared with his boa constrictor. 'Would you like a photograph with my snake?' It took every ounce of my powers of persuasion to convince Emma not to throw up in her lap (and I had to pay the snake-handler to move along a few blocks). I once told her about Sam, the snake of my childhood, and she nearly left me. Here in Miami, there's a black racer that lives in our garden – residing in the shrubbery at the north-east corner of the property. We have been living in this house for two years, and I still haven't told her about it. If I did, I suspect we would be on the next plane back to London.

My fear is more bound to context. When I'm running with Hugo, I rationalize. There are forty-five species of snake found in Florida, only six of which are poisonous. So I tell myself, with admittedly sloppy logic, the chances are 13-2 against any snake we encounter on our run being venomous. Actually, it is better than that – there are only four species of poisonous snake in this part of south Florida. And within each species, the numbers of venomous snakes are relatively sparse compared to the non-venomous ones. So the odds are heavily slanted in my favour anyway. I know this. In addition, most snakes in the vicinity, poisonous or not, will hear my leaden-footed thudding and skedaddle off into the undergrowth. I know this too. If I do manage to get myself bitten by a poisonous snake it may inject little or no venom. And even if I get the full monty, it's overwhelmingly likely that I'm going to survive. I know all this. But when I hear the tell-tale rustling of a snake that is somewhere nearby but I can't be sure quite where, then all that I know evaporates before my eyes, disappearing in a little puff of irrelevant smoke.

When I was growing up in Wales, in addition to Boots, I had another companion: a garter snake who hailed from the US and whom I, accordingly, baptized Sam. Boots was not entirely enamoured, but I liked Sam, and so I tended to give him the run of the house. Sometimes he would disappear for days on end. When he reappeared, it would almost invariably be at my mother's expense – she'd be doing something like rooting through the cupboard in search of a can of something or other, and out he would spring (or so she alleged). My mother was actually quite fond of Sam too. But when a snake pokes his little head out at you as you are rummaging through a cupboard, then your heart rate is going to shoot from seventy to seven million and there's nothing you can do about it. No matter how much you suspect Sam is going to be there – no matter how much you rationalize the situation – when he does appear, something basic and biological takes over; and it really doesn't care about your rationalizations. That is how I feel about snakes. When the high-frequency pitter-pat rustling of a lizard on the leaves gives way to the languid rustle of a snake, my scrotum attempts to beat a rapid retreat up inside my abdomen as if to say: take the husk, but spare the gene line. Spare what is immortal in this body. And then all I am aware of is fear – visceral, irrational and overwhelming. That is what I have done my best to bequeath Hugo.

After about a mile or so of generally low-grade anxiety (occasionally escalating to soaring panic), the forest opens out into grassland. Here is a small lake where Hugo can cool down, after I've checked for gators and moccasins. Both are ubiquitous in south Florida, and you always have to keep a wary eye open. But I've never seen any at this particular watering hole, and I think the definite danger of overheating has precedence over the potential danger of a passing reptile. So Hugo wades around in the water – I won't let him swim here – while I scan the surface for movement; tense, on my toes, ready for action. A few minutes later we are on our way again, Hugo reinvigorated, bounding ahead of me as he knows I will now allow him to do. There is an old road here, and I can – usually – see far enough along it to recognize the outline of any snake that might be sunning itself.

We see snakes here almost every day, but most are harmless. Black racers are everywhere. There is a big orange ratsnake we sometimes glimpse in the dead grass that lines the trail. And there is an improbably long and thin coachwhip we occasionally find basking on the cracked and faded tarmac. That snake is an admirably phlegmatic character – once, when I first discovered this place, in the twilight days of Nina and Tess, I wasn't looking out as carefully as I should and Nina walked right over the top of him. But when he does decide to move, boy is that snake fast! I doubt I could catch him, even if I tried.

Encounters with poisonous snakes are, thankfully, rare. There are the moccasins I've already mentioned: sometimes known as the cottonmouth – when alarmed, it opens its jaws wide and the inside of its mouth is pure cotton-white. Moccasins are a species of pit viper – so called because of the hole or 'pit' that can be seen between their eyes and their nose, which contains the heat detectors that these vipers use to identify and locate prey. In this part of the world, you will find no shortage of people ready to regale you with stories of just how aggressive, almost diabolical, is the moccasin. I suspect this has much to do with the fact that they just look so utterly evil. There are no beautiful markings, as on some of the other local venomous serpents. Their bodies are black and fat, almost bloated looking if the snake is healthy, and the head is often a lighter shade – like a brown skull. I have not yet seen a moccasin in south Florida, but I saw plenty when I lived in Alabama. There, they could be a little problematic during breeding season – April and May – soon after they have woken up from their hibernation (in south Florida, they don't hibernate). But in general, at least in my experience, they were relatively placid. Also, while they have been known to travel miles from water, it is quite unusual for them to do so. So while I have to keep a keen eye open for them when Hugo goes swimming, once we have left the lake behind there are other snakes more worthy of worry.

Here, everyone is afraid of coral snakes, largely because they are members of the cobra family. Brightly banded in red, black and yellow, they are easily mistaken for the harmless kingsnake. You have to look closely at the order of banding: red touching black, friend of Jack; red touching yellow, kill a fellow. Of course, with my markedly failing eyesight, I suspect that the inspection needed to identify this information would have to be done from uncomfortably close range and, all things considered, I think it would probably be better to just run the other way. The venom of the coral snake is neurotoxic – it attacks the nervous system, and death is the result of asphyxiation – whereas the venom of all the other poisonous serpents of Florida is haemotoxic – it attacks the red blood cells. Neurotoxic venom is more deadly, but does not come with the wish-I-would-hurry-up-and-die sort of pain associated with haemotoxic venom – or so I am told. If you're bitten by a coral snake, Floridians tell me, you'll be dead in thirty minutes. In fact, this is exaggerated. First of all, death is by no means guaranteed. It all depends on where they bite you, how much venom they inject and how long it takes the nearest anti-venom team to reach you. Secondly, for poorly understood reasons, it can sometimes take hours for the symptoms of coral snake envenomization to occur. The first symptom is a sore throat, followed by an inability to keep one's eyelids open – not because you can't stay awake but simply because your eyelids won't do what you tell them. If this happens, you need help fast – but as long as you get it your chances are still very good.

Pygmy rattlers actually worry me a lot more than coral snakes or moccasins. There are no timber rattlers this far south, but its smaller cousin – they rarely grow beyond two feet or so – the pygmy, or dusky pygmy, rattler is an aggressive little sod, the Napoleon of the snake world. They don't move aside when they hear you coming; and they are useless at warning you of their presence – a rather unfortunate combination. Their rattle is small and often so faint that it sounds more like a cricket than a rattlesnake. The venom of their bite also belies their small stature. Their bite is unlikely to be fatal, at least not for me, but is nevertheless extremely painful.

But today's run is going to be special. We are going to see something that we may well never see again. On the road in front of us, sunning itself, unconcerned, in the morning heat, is perhaps the most singularly impressive snake in North America: an eastern diamondback rattler. Diamondbacks are truly beautiful animals. Their name comes from the pattern of wedges that runs all the way along their body, forming a latticework of diamonds, dark brown around the edges and beige inside – brown and beige, the colours of the 1970s, my childhood, my home. Hugo and I stand and look, just for a while, and then run on.

This is a story of snakes, and fathers, and of a home to which I can never return. There is a reason why Satan chose to appear to Eve in the form of a serpent. There is a reason he did not choose to appear as a rabbit or a bird, a squirrel or a bug.

In the beginning there was darkness on the face of the deep and the world was without form and void. But then God the Father said, 'Let there be light!' and there was light. And He saw that it was good. A neat trick, you might think, but how did He pull it off? Light is, of course, energy, and in creating energy, God — our ingenuity has subsequently allowed us to discover — employed two principles: the first and second laws of thermodynamics. According to the first law, energy can neither be created nor destroyed, merely converted from one form into another. According to the second law, any closed system tends towards the maximum disorder.

If we were closed systems, then we would tend to the maximum disorder. This means we would soon cease to exist. Complex structures, like you and I, are ordered: our complexity is a measure of our order. The more disordered a system, the less complex it is. A maximally disordered system is one that has broken down into its constituent particles. This is the destiny of all closed systems. 'Entropy' is the name scientists give to disorder. To avoid the ravages of entropy we need energy. This is what the second law tells us. But the first law tells us that we cannot simply create this energy from nothing. We need to get it from somewhere else — or, more precisely, from something else. And so, like any living thing, I am an energy converter: I take something else's energy and make it my own.

Think of what God did when He said, 'Let there be light!' and chose to implement this injunction through the laws of thermodynamics. In that instant, the world He will go on to create is destined to be a zero-sum competition for energy. The first law makes it zero-sum: since energy can be neither created nor destroyed (presumably this applies only after the initial act of creation), there is only a certain amount of energy and no more. And anything that wants to avoid the depredations of the second law must take in energy from other things that have it – and it must do this by breaking those things down, and so appropriating the energy they contain. Complexity is order, and order is a defiance of the second law. We are all minor out-laws. We live in defiance of the Law. We live on borrowed time and stolen energy. Ever since God said, 'Let there be light!' the universe has been a brutal, unforgiving place.

The laws of thermodynamics shape all living things, and they have one clear consequence: the fundamental design structure of most living things is the tube. The reason is not difficult to discern. The tube is the energy-conversion device par excellence. Plants are stationary tubes; animals are mobile ones. For those tubes that became animals, energy, in the form of structured living matter, goes in at one end. The matter is broken down, the energy released and the waste products excreted at the other end. From a design point of view, the tube is the simplest way of satisfying this require-ment. A zoologist from another universe, where we can suppose the two laws do not apply, might justifiably classify most earthly fauna as subspecies of worm. We are super-structures built on and around our alimentary canal – on and around the worm that we once were.

Before he was cast to earth, Satan was Morning Star, the most beautiful of the angels. Lucifer is Latin for 'Bringer of light'. But to be cast to earth is to become subject to the first and second laws of thermodynamics – the fundamental laws of the earth. Morning Star, the bringer of light, is transformed from producer to exchanger of energy. It had to be a serpent in the Garden of Eden, because Morning Star had to become a tube. When Satan appeared to Eve in the form of a serpent, he was both medium and message. His form simply reminded us of something we have tried to forget. Our fine bodily clothes are draped around the frame of a worm. We can almost forget this, but the evidence just keeps seeping out.

The worms of life become more and more complex: more and more impressive bodily frames become built on and around the worm. This, too, is a consequence of the laws of thermodynamics. One worm tries to eat another and so appropriate its energy. The other worm develops a defensive shell – a carapace – to prevent its being eaten. The first worm develops mechanisms – teeth, claws – to break down the carapace. The other worm develops a more robust carapace, or means of locomotion to escape those teeth and claws. And so life unfolds.

But, then, something strange and unexpected happens. Some of the worms – or what the worms have become as the result of this arms race – reach a certain threshold level of complexity and become conscious. No one is entirely sure how or when this happened. But it did happen. Was it a blessing or a curse?

The two laws of thermodynamics entail that death and destruction are built into the process of life, as essential elements of that process. One organism can live only if another dies. A universe designed by way of these laws will be a montage of destruction. However, until consciousness – in the form of animals – developed, there was no suffering in this universe: there was nothing capable of suffering. A living thing – like a plant or very simple animal – that is not conscious can be damaged and it can die. But it cannot suffer because suffering is consciousness of this damage and this dying. It is consciousness that brings both suffering and enjoyment to the world. If the enjoyment it brings outweighs the suffering, then I don't think anyone would deny that it was a blessing. However, it is difficult to see how consciousness could do this given the sort of universe in which it developed.

The nineteenth-century philosopher Arthur Schopenhauer – usually thought of as German although he was actually born in Gdansk, in what is now Poland – saw this more clearly than anyone else. Even though he knew nothing about the laws of thermodynamics, and the idea of a zero-sum competition for energy was one that he did not consider, his view of the universe was similar to the one I have just sketched. Given the sort of universe in which it developed, Schopenhauer thought, it was inevitable that consciousness should introduce more suffering than enjoyment: 'A quick test of the assertion that enjoyment outweighs pain in this world, or that they are at any rate balanced, would be to compare the feelings of an animal engaged in eating another with those of the animal being eaten.' Consciousness is not, itself, a bad thing. But it has arisen in a bad universe: a universe designed according to the laws of thermodynamics.

When the descendants of worms reach a certain level of complexity – and so become conscious – then each is able to consciously discriminate how it is faring in the competition for energy. Roughly, the sign that the battle goes well is called 'enjoyment' or 'pleasure'; and the indication that it is going badly is called 'suffering' or 'pain'. When the battle is going well, then as long as nothing changes it will keep going well. But when the battle is going badly, this needs to be addressed – because soon there will be no further opportunities for the battle to go at all, well or badly. Therefore, the consciousness of the children of the worm needs to be far more sensitive to a battle for energy that is going badly than one that is going well. And so, in the life of any conscious creature, if it is not extraordinarily lucky, it is likely that its suffering will outweigh its enjoyment: that the pain it experiences in the course of its life will overshadow the pleasure.

That is why we never really notice when things are going well. My snarling right Achilles tendon – it went to sleep for the last couple of miles, but has now woken up in a foul mood – makes this point for me in a painfully unambiguous way. I am utterly oblivious to just how well everything else is going. It's all relative, of course, but my heart is still beating nicely, my lungs are still doing a passable job of inhaling and expelling air and, the one Achilles tendon aside, the remainder of my legs are still doing what they are supposed to without any complaints. So all in all, my body is doing a good job. But do I notice this? Do I feel any sense of gratitude that things are going so well? Of course not, as Schopenhauer realized:

> Just as a stream flows smoothly as long as it encounters no obstruction, so the nature of man and animal is such that we never really notice or become conscious of what is agreeable to our will. If we are to notice something, our will has to have been thwarted, or to have experienced a shock of some kind. On the other hand, all that opposes,

frustrates and resists our will, that is to say all that is unpleasant and painful, impresses itself on us instantly, directly, and with great clarity.

Our consciousness, or awareness, is inevitably going to be far more concerned with things that are going wrong in our lives rather than things that are going right. That my heart is beating efficiently as I run is not something that needs to be addressed. As long as things don't change, it will continue beating efficiently, and so there is nothing I need do about it. But the vociferous Achilles tendon does need to be addressed, even if addressing here means nothing more than turning my attention to it and making a judgement about what to do – continue with the run, stretch it out or maybe even stop. If it is not addressed, then it might rupture and that will be curtains for my life of running. Bad things need to be addressed, but good things do not. That is why consciousness will tend to focus on the bad.

For humans, Schopenhauer argues, the situation is further exacerbated by our relatively sophisticated cognitive abilities, especially the ability to remember past events and anticipate future ones:

The chief source of all this passion is that thought for what is absent and future, which, with man, exercises such a powerful influence upon all he does. It is this that is the real origin of his cares, his hopes, his fears – emotions which affect him much more deeply than could ever be the case with those present joys and sufferings to which the brute is confined. In his powers of reflection, memory and foresight, man possesses, as it were, a machine for condensing and storing up his pleasures and sorrows.

Schopenhauer is, here, building on his argument concerning more basic forms of consciousness. Suppose we accept that consciousness will tend to focus heavily on things going badly rather than things going well. Memory and anticipation are just relatively sophisticated forms of consciousness. Therefore it would make sense for them, too, to be concerned predominantly with the bad rather than the good. Our memory and anticipation would tend to favour the malign rather than the benign so that we can prevent these occurrences from happening again (memory) or prevent them from happening at all (anticipation). When consciousness becomes progressively more sophisticated, the imbalance of suffering and enjoyment becomes progressively more accentuated. Life is bad for all living things, but it is – all other things being equal, which humans will go out of their way to ensure they never are – worst of all for humans.

Schopenhauer claimed that the story of The Fall is the one thing that reconciled him to the Old Testament because it was the 'sole metaphysical truth' contained in that book. He did not believe in the literal truth of this story. Neither do I. Schopenhauer, perhaps more keenly than anyone, understood that the most important truths always appear clothed in allegory and that the most important part of the story is not what it appears to be about, but rather what you find reluctantly crawling out from between each line. In these stories – of Creation and Fall – we need to distinguish the literal truth or falsity of the story from what, following Schopenhauer, we can call its 'metaphysical' truth: 'For they lead us to the insight that, like the children of libertine fathers, we come into the world already encumbered with guilt and that it is only because we have to atone for this guilt that our existence is so wretched and its end is death ... For our existence resembles nothing so much as the consequence of a misdeed, punishment for a forbidden desire.'

If God is all-good, all-powerful and all-knowing, He can do whatever He wants to do, and doesn't make mistakes. So why would He have created a universe designed in accordance with the laws of thermodynamics? These laws guarantee that the resulting universe will be a zero-sum panorama of destruction and death. They guarantee that, should consciousness ever arise in this universe, suffering will always have the upper hand on happiness. They guarantee that while life is bad for all living things, it will be worst of all for the, self-styled, 'highest specimens'. If this is all the work of the Father, then why would He do this to his creation? The most obvious explanation – and it seems difficult to imagine another explanation – is that He is punishing us for our misdeeds. If there were a God, and He created us, then we could be pretty sure that He has pulled up the ladder and sealed shut the gates of heaven. The Father, it seems, does not like his children very much at all.

This is monstrously sad. There is a good reason why Schopenhauer became known as the philosopher of pessimism. But what I find most interesting and instructive about Schopenhauer is not his description of the human predicament – in which I think he is largely correct. It is his response. This is, to say the least, unexpected. When people think of Schopenhauer, they won't think of this response at all. But I've come to think it is the most important thing Schopenhauer ever said.

Imagine you are on a seriously unpleasant bus ride. The road is little more than a dirt track, sprinkled with potholes, and you are constantly bounced around in your seat. This seat is nothing more than a wooden plank, and your backside is getting more and more bruised as the journey continues. There is no air-conditioning and you are uncomfortably hot, sweat is dripping down your back and you are starting to smell. But this is nothing compared to the people around you: a reeking, belching, farting, pestilential quorum of humanity. Many of them have brought livestock and other animals along with them on the journey. Kids are screaming, nappies are being changed in front of your eyes. The toilet is blocked and overflowing, and people and animals are pissing and defecating in the aisle. It is clear that no one on the bus, including you, has any idea where you're going and only the haziest idea of where you are coming from. Nevertheless, all around you people are making up ridiculous stories, lacking any sort of grounding in logic, evidence or even satisfying narrative theme, of where it is they are going to alight and their prospects once they have done so.

Then, out of the corner of your eye, you catch someone looking at you and you look back. In their eyes, you see the same anguish; the same recognition of hopelessness and futility, the same disgust, the same fear. And, at that moment, you realize that you are both in this together. And this realization quickly extends to all of your fellow passengers. They are perhaps not as lucid or aware as the person who caught your eye, but it is all a matter of degree. You realize that to some extent or other – some more, some less – everyone on the bus understands his or her wretchedness. The silly stories they tell each other are fuelled by confusion and terror. The realization is like a bolt between the eyes. And so you realize you can forgive your fellow passengers for what you have regarded as their flaws. They are scared and bewildered, shocked and disgusted, just like you. The only reasonable attitude to your fellow passengers is tolerance, patience and solicitude. It is what they both need and deserve.

This, in effect, was the conclusion Schopenhauer reached from his reflections on the nature of the world:

> In fact, the conviction that the world and man is something that had better not have been, is of a kind to fill us with indulgence towards one another. Nay, from this point of view, we might well consider the proper form of address to be, not *Monsieur, Sir, Mein Herr*, but *my fellow-sufferer, Soci malorum, compagnon de misères*. This may sound strange, but it is in keeping with the facts; it puts others in the right light; and it reminds us of that which is after all the most necessary thing in life – the tolerance, patience, regard and love of neighbour, of which everyone stands in need, and which, therefore, every man owes his fellow.

The crucial question, however, is one that Schopenhauer didn't appear to even consider: in a world that is a zero-sum competition for energy, how are things like tolerance, patience, compassion and love even possible?

I have returned home from my run with Hugo and my meta-physical speculations are interrupted by more earthly and immediate concerns. So here I am, a new daddy, staring down the barrel of fifty: tired, sweaty, back from the run and with duties to perform. Brenin is nearly two years old. Macsen is two weeks old. Both of them have nappies that need changing. The energy goes in, the energy comes out. For the last two years and for the next two at least, my earthly existence has been crushing testament to this consequence of the two laws of thermodynamics, the fundamental design principles of life.

I love my sons in a way that is difficult to put into words; or even into thoughts – at the moment I just don't have the distance to do this. The love started at a few weeks of age. I would like to say that it was love at first sight – that I loved my sons and wanted to hold on to them tight and never let them go from the moment I first saw them – but that wouldn't be entirely true. After my first son was born I spent the next couple of weeks or so in shock; and the prospect of having to hold on to him, tight or otherwise, occasioned fear and trembling rather than love. But then he did something to me, something unkind and, I can't help but think, ruthlessly calculating. In fact, they each did the same thing around the same time – when they were a few weeks old. They smiled at me. They smiled at me – and I've been their bitch ever since.

But that is just an expression I use to denote my inability to write and think about what I do feel. That's just my way of saying – and this is just another crude, overtly macho, metaphor – I love them so much I'd gladly take a bullet for them if there was one around that needed taking. But where does love fit into the view of the universe sketched by Schopenhauer? In a zero-sum competition for energy, what place is there for love?

Love is a funny little puzzle. First of all, love is clearly compatible with the two laws of thermodynamics. After all, love came into existence in a universe built around those laws. Love is therefore compatible with the laws in the sense that they clearly do not rule it out. But sometimes in a sporting event, when someone does something that is, by the rules of the game, legal but questionable, people say that what he or she did was not in the spirit of the game. Love might have stuck to the letter of the law, but there is something about it that seems to have ridden roughshod over the spirit of the great game of life. The most obvious consequence of the two laws of thermodynamics is that life will be a zero-sum competition for energy. And then somehow, with stunning improbability, love insinuated its way in too. How can something so brazenly opposed to the spirit of a zero-sum competition for energy have emerged from that competition?

To protect themselves and the energy that was the currency of the great game of life, some of the children of the worm developed a hardened carapace. Those who would steal their energy developed teeth. Others developed methods of loco-motion to escape those who would steal their energy. Those who would take their energy developed legs to chase and claws to catch. Then, at some point, some of the children formed groups; either to more effectively protect themselves from those who would take their energy or to more effectively hunt those whose energy they would take. This turned out to be an effective and stable evolutionary strategy.

These groups began small: a circle of parents and chil-dren, no more. In some of the children of worms, the groups became larger. But, whatever their size, we must remember why they happened in the first place. An individual creature was more likely to survive, and so pass on its genes, if it was a member of the group. The group benefited the individuals that made it up – the individuals and their genes. That was the sole evolutionary justification of the group.

This leads to a problem. Suppose you have a group of indi-viduals, all of whom, ultimately, are in the group to benefit themselves. On the face of it, the group is likely to be an unstable enterprise, scarred by rifts, quarrels and conflicts of interest. How do you hold the group together? In some crea-tures – ants, termites and bees are good examples – even wondrously large social groups are held together by subtle chemical signals. But some of the children of worms became entirely different sorts of creature. They became sentient, capable of feeling. And these creatures were fertile ground for an entirely different evolutionary strategy. These creatures, through random mutation and natural selection, became fond of each other.

There was more to it than that. Even if some of the children became fond of each other, and acted accordingly, evolution still had to deal with those who, for whatever reason, did not always feel what they were supposed to feel and so did not always toe the line. The role of sanction – of penalties of increasing orders of severity up to and including expulsion from the group or death – plays a significant part in holding the group together. But when we look at some of the more recently developed children of worms, mammalian social groups – coyotes, wolves, monkeys and apes, even human apes – then it is simply false to say that these groups are held together only by the threat of sanction. A human society held together only by this threat would be a society of sociopaths. Perhaps certain criminal fraternities approximate this condition, though I suspect that most do not. But it is clear that this provides a wildly erroneous model of human societies in general. For most of us non-sociopaths, it is natural – biologically natural – for us to like each other: to feel affection and concern for each other, to enjoy the presence of the others, to feel pleasure in their company and sorrow in their absence. All this is natural: the absence of these feelings is an indication that something has gone wrong on a basic biological level. These feelings – these social instincts, as Darwin put it – are the glue that holds together groups of social mammals. These feelings of affection, therefore, make an animal better equipped to compete in the zero-sum competition for energy.

While these feelings – affection, compassion, love – might adhere to the letter of the laws of thermodynamics, there is something in them that is just so inimical to their spirit. The love I feel for my sons is, from an evolutionary point of view, the easiest to explain: I love my sons because they carry my genes. My resulting behaviour biologists call 'kin altruism'. Evolution equipped me with these feelings because they made it more likely that my genes would continue: it is the propagation of my genes that provides the selection pressure that explains both the origin of this kind of love and also what keeps this kind of love in existence. This claim is true, but has led many people to draw illegitimate inferences. Understanding this is crucial to understanding the way in which love can outstrip the laws that made it.

Some people think this means I do not really love my sons, but only their genes. There are two confusions embodied in this idea. First, there is a logical fallacy – what is known as the 'genetic fallacy'. The claim that I really only love my genes confuses the origin of my love – what my love derives from – with the content of my love; that is, with what my love is love of. This distinction between the origin and content of an emotion is a distinction between what causes an emotion or feeling, and the object of that emotion or feeling. This distinction is a quite general one, applying not only to love but to all emotions. So, for example, my tiredness might cause me to be angry with someone. Tiredness is the origin of my anger – if I had not been so tired, their behaviour would not have made me angry. However, it is still true that I am angry with them – I am not, in this case, angry at my tiredness (although in other circumstances, I might be angry with that too). To explain the origin of love is to explain what caused love – how love came into being (and also why it is still around today). To give an account of the content of love is to identify the object that love has – what this love is love of. It may be true that I love my sons because of the genes they carry. That is an account of the origin of my love. This origin lies in a biological strategy, based on the premise that fathers like me that love their sons will tend, statistically, to have more sons reaching maturity – and so be in a position to pass on their genes – than fathers that do not. So, all things being equal, evolution would favour the genes of fathers like me. Nevertheless, to suppose this means that I really love my genes and not my sons would be to confuse the origin and content of my love. My genes might be the cause of my love, but the objects of my love are still my sons. It is still true, therefore, that I love my sons and not my genes.

In addition to confusing the origin of love with the content of love, the idea that I really love my genes and not my sons falls victim to another confusion: the idea that we are slaves to unconscious processes driven or dictated by genes. In effect, the idea assumes that my genes are smarter than I am. But my genes have no idea how much I know. The body is the husk, but the gene line is immortal. This is the great myth concerning the idea that my sons carry my genes. The idea of an immortal coil carried within me, passed on to my sons and to their children and their children's children is simply false. For a start, to point out the obvious, it is not true that, as I am sometimes told, my sons carry half of my genes. I share between 94 and 98 per cent of my genes with any given chimpanzee and, preliminary indications suggest, over 90 per cent of them with any given dog. How curious that I should share over 90 per cent of my genes with Hugo but only half of my genes with my sons. What I, in fact, share with my sons, is not 50 per cent of the genes that comprise me, but roughly 50 per cent of the genes that can vary from one human to another – a tiny, tiny portion of my overall genetic code. As for the genes that do not vary from one human to another – they play a role in making me a human in the basic biological sense, that's all. They do not, in any way, make me the individual person that I am for the simple reason that I share these genes with all other humans. There is no reason for me to love these genes. They are certainly not the sorts of thing for which I am going to take a bullet.

So if there are any genes that are candidates for objects of my love they are going to be restricted to a vanishingly small portion of my overall genetic code, the ones that can vary from human to human and play a role in making me the individual person I am. What happens to those genes? It is not as if my sons carry all of these genes peculiar to me – the idiosyncratic genes inside of me. Roughly 50 per cent of these idiosyncratic genes will have come from Emma. My already tiny immortal contribution has immediately dwindled by half. If my sons go on to have children – biologically, the best-case scenario for my genes – my contribution will then have dwindled by approximately 75 per cent. Soon – in cosmic terms, the blink of an eye – my genetic contribution is going to asymptotically approach zero. Why would I love this ever-decreasing and soon to be effectively zero genetic contribution? I would have to be pretty stupid, really. Sometimes people assume that if a trait or tendency is genetic, it is immune from subsequent interference or amendment by way of processes of rational inference. That assumption is simply mistaken.

*

A little more than half a lifetime ago I spent some time in India. Not much, just a few months when the university was in summer recess. My movements were hampered by a rather stubborn case of bacillary dysentery. For three days before getting on a bus or train, I had to completely starve myself. Dysentery is not like a normal case of diarrhoea just ratcheted up a few notches; you have no effective control over your bowels at all – a few seconds grace is all you have. Only if there was absolutely, positively nothing in me did I dare venture more than ten feet or so from a toilet. Most of what I remember about India is hotel ceilings: lying on beds staring up at ceilings and waiting, waiting for the worm around which I had been built to empty itself of its energy.

One day I found myself on one of these malnourished bus trips to somewhere or other – I think I was still in the state of Jammu and Kashmir, or possibly in Himachal Pradesh, but I have no memory of where I was going or where I had come from. I saw something of which I thought little at the time, but the memory lay coiled inside me waiting until its time came – waiting until I became a father. We had stopped in a village somewhere in the mountains. The people from the bus, all strangers to me, were buying lunch from the roadside vendors, something that my intestinal challenges precluded. So I took a little stroll to the edge of the village. There was a group of monkeys, maybe forty of them, sitting at the side of the road where the village met the forest – little, grey, pink-faced *bandars*, Rhesus macaques as we know them. And, in the middle of a small congregation of four or five, one monkey was embracing a puppy. The bandar held him in his arms and hugged him close. Occasionally one of the other monkeys from the congregation would lean over and pat the puppy, an open-handed pat-pat-pat on the ribs, just as a human might pat their dog. The bandar held the puppy in his arms, and every now and the puppy would lick his pink face.

When my first son smiled at me, the love I felt was decisively shaped by a certain type of recognition. It was not that I recognized my genes in his smile – genes that had somehow been hidden in his scowls, gas-fuelled grimaces and blank stares. Rather, in his smile I recognized utter helplessness, but also the beginnings – nascent, halting and as yet uncertain – of trust. Life can crush him in a heartbeat; but it can do the same to me too. The differences between us are of degree, not kind. Indeed, in the end life will crush us both. After a promising but ultimately misleading start, life will chew us up and spit us out. We have been thrown into a bad place, abandoned in a strange land built on evil principles. And in his smile I saw this abandonment echoing down through the ages. This love is grounded in mutual recognition. In the end, under the gaze of eternity, I am just a monkey who has found a puppy, and I will love it and hold on tight as long as I can. But the trust, the nascent trust – well, that's just the most heartbreaking of all. You should not trust me, my sons. I know the world. I'll do the best I can. But in the end, in my most important duty of protection, I shall always fail you. I'm just not good enough. I cannot save you. No one can.

Let me tell you a story, my sons, now that your nappies have been changed and before you go to sleep. Once, before you were born and in a place you have never been, my thoughts played a game with themselves. I called it the 'I am built on something much older' game. The game was interrupted, and I've only now been able to finish it.

Once upon a time there was a worm that dressed himself

up in fine clothes and told splendid stories about himself. So fine were the clothes, and so splendid were the stories, he almost – almost – succeeded in forgetting that he was a worm. But he couldn't quite do it; the evidence just kept coming out. Every full diaper is a confession.

We are worms – you and I – and, in the end, we shall be eaten by worms. Our immortal coil is not deoxyribonucleic acid (DNA). We are created in the image of the laws of thermodynamics, and our immortal coil is the worm. But for a brief time we have an opportunity to become more than this. When we love, we become more than worms: to love is to reject the laws that made us. Of course, we must stick to the letter of these laws; but we can nonetheless reject their spirit. The laws cannot be broken but sometimes, just sometimes, they can be bent.

To love is to defy the history that made us. Love is the acknowledgement that any living thing is of bad blood – the product of flawed design principles. Love is the acknowledgement that there is a bad end in store for all of us – that we are temporary aberrations that soon will be erased by the rising tide of entropy. But it is simultaneously the realization that we are all in this together. Love is the realization that every living sentient thing both needs and deserves our sympathy and our patience. Every act of kindness we show to someone or something is a defiance of the spirit of the laws that made us. When we cherish what is good over what is evil, this is a defiance of the spirit of the laws that made us. Life, in the final analysis, is a temporary upsurge in a universe ill-equipped for it, a transient incongruity. Heat death is the universe's final, and indeed normal, state. Life is a defiance of the law. And the fact that this defiance is futile does not make it any less valuable.

But, my sons, my puppies of heavy diapers, *mes compagnons de misères*: you are beautiful. To this particular monkey you will always be little gods – my little gods who shit. And yes, of course, even a monkey knows that, logically, a god cannot defecate. God would not steal energy to stay in existence – and therefore God would not have ends. Anything that does has a dependent existence: it needs something else in order to maintain itself in being. Its existence is, therefore, not absolute – not the existence proper to any god worthy of the title. But what do I care of logic when I look in your faces and see only life and hope, delight and trust? Logic preaches acquiescence. Logic breathes compliance. But it is only our defiance that redeems us, because our defiance is inseparable from our love. If there is indeed a God who made us, then all love is a war on God.

6

The *Digue*
2010

I'm running along the *digue*: a dyke that runs across much of the delta of the River Orb in the Languedoc region of France and was built to discourage the storm surges of the winter Mediterranean. To the south of the *digue* lies the *maïre*, and after that the beach. Already, young families are starting to make their way down there, to a place of life and warmth and the echoing laughter of the children of summer.

I first came to this place with my father when I was a boy and he was still a relatively young man. And, no matter where it has taken me in between, my life always seems to return here: keeps bringing me back, offering me one excuse, then another, that I just can't seem to refuse. Now I'm a father, still relatively young, or so I tell myself. A little more than a decade ago, I carried rocks from this place to bury a wolf that I had come to think of as my brother. The memories of a boy with his father, of a young man with his dead wolf brother, of a man growing old fast whom life has brought back to this place once again – that these memories should belong to a single life strikes me as stunningly improbable. But whose memories would they be if not mine?

On the land side of the *digue*, there are abandoned vineyards. The winter Mediterranean does not really care too much about our efforts to discourage it and, two or three times in a winter, water will surge over the *digue*. Where the vines once grew is now bitter, broken ground. The houses of those who once worked the grapes are derelict, and there remain only the broken lines of vines, withered and blasted, mixed with the increasingly triumphant smatterings of cord grass and marsh samphire.

The idea of a line, in some form or other, often decisively shapes the way we think of time. We talk of 'time's arrow', or we think of time as a river – perhaps even as a man and his dog running along a dyke from the past into an unknown future. The fact that we use metaphors that are spatial suggests that we don't really understand time very well at all. Physicists, on the other hand, tell us that time is an expression of entropy: that the direction of time follows the direction of increasing entropy. I am not sure that physicists understand time any better than the rest of us. But, even so, there are very different metaphors associated with the account physics provides. Entropy is disorder, and so time is a transformation of order into disorder. And, armed with this, we might think of time as a series of waves, storm surges; washing in, retreating, and repeating over and over again. Each time the surge retreats, it leaves less and less of what was there before. When I first came to this place, the vines were young and green, and bent over with the weight of the grapes they carried. But the surges of time have done their work, and this is what remains. Soon, what is left of these vineyards will have returned to the *maïre*.

The *Digue*

It is not time's arrows but time's surges that break us down. In the end, we all return to the *maïre*.

Hugo and I are on a fifteen-mile circuit of the Orb delta. We all arrived here from Miami a couple of months ago. In Miami in summer, or the hurricane and humidity festival that passes for a summer in those parts, six miles is enough to nearly kill us, and we don't get much change out of an hour. But we're beasting this run. We both struggled initially with the extra distance, but two months later we're doing these fifteen miles in two hours thirty, give or take. It's not exactly cold, of course. This is the south of France in June, and it's probably only a few degrees below the temperature in Miami when we left – but the dry air feels wonderful. Hugo is so cocky he's even putting in some extra miles, dashing off to meet the white horses and black bulls that line the edges of the fields as we pass. Hugo is not a particularly brave dog and I smirk at his fawning approaches. Not so many years ago, I ran here with somewhat different animals.

We began running west along the beach, and then turned north along the edge of the *rivierette*, a small saltwater lagoon. Then west again for a couple of miles along the *digue*, over as far as the *digue* will go, to the Grande Maïre, the massive saltwater lagoon from which the *rivierette* was born a few centuries ago, the result it is thought of subsidence. Turning north along its densely bullrushed banks, we run for a few more miles, water on one side, fields and then vineyards on the other – the hills of the Massif Central shimmering in the hot distance that lies to the front of us. Then we'll hook up with the Canal du Midi, the incredible engineering legacy of Pierre-Paul Riquet, Béziers' most famous son. The canal stretches over 150 miles, from the

Garonne river in the west to the Etang de Thau some thirty miles east of us. We head along the canal for only a few of those miles, west towards Villeneuve-lès-Béziers, shaded from the growing sun by the mighty sycamores that line its banks. Then, continuing on the dirt tracks through the vineyards to Sérignan, we head down to the beach and a turn to the east that takes us back home.

But these are all just contingencies: distances, directions, times, even landscape. They don't matter. The heartbeat of the run is the essence of the run, what the run really is. Here, on an early summer's morning in Languedoc, the heartbeat is a gentle one. There is the gentle sinking of my feet into sandy ground, the gentle pant-pant-pant of Hugo's breath and the quiet jingle-jingle-jingle of the tags that adorn his collar. There is the whispering rustle of the *tramontane* – the wind of the mountains – in the branches of the sycamores above me and in the vines that surround me. There is the gentle dance of the butterflies in the warm breeze. When the run does its work, I will become lost in its beating heart. We run on.

I remember another run, along some of these same trails, but in a different time, almost a different life. Brenin had lymphoma, the vet had told me, and the prognosis was what in the profession they call 'guarded'. In other words, he was going to die. It was going to be soon and my primary duty now, the last important thing I could do for my old friend, was to make his death as easy as it could be. As easy as it could be for him, I mean. That probably meant making it hard for me. If he could just slip away in the night, painlessly, unaware ... But I suspected that was not the way it was going to be. Not since Max II had any dog of mine slipped away in their sleep and I had been six years old at the time. I was going to have to make a decision, a final judgement. The judgement would be that Brenin's life was no longer worth living. Not a second less of a life worth living, and not a second more of a life that was not. That was the goal. Then I would have to take him to the vet, and I would have to ask the vet to kill him. I am human. I make mistakes. My decision would always be riddled with doubt. Even now, years later, I ask myself: was that the right day? Did I get it right? Was it too soon? Or was I too slow, too late – too weak? These are questions I have never been able to answer and probably never will.

We had just returned from taking Nina and Tess to boarding kennels for a few days. They were still young then, exhausting to be around; and I had decided Brenin might benefit from a short rest, a break from their grinding effervescence. Upon our return, I quickly noticed a change in Brenin's demeanour. Brighter, more alert, more interested, hungrier than he had been in weeks – I offered him the spaghetti I had made for my lunch and he quickly devoured it. Then he did something altogether unexpected. He jumped onto the sofa and howled.

When he was a young wolf, Brenin had a little party piece that he would perform most days. He would run full-tilt at the settee, jump onto it and then continue his run up the wall. When he had got as high as his momentum would carry him, which was typically around three-quarters of the way up a standard living-room wall, he would spin his back legs up and around – a kind of canine cartwheel – and then run back down the wall. This was his way of letting me know we had been dawdling in the house for far too long, and that it was time for a run. Time had stripped him of this sort of outrageous athleticism – jumping on the settee and howling

137

had become his middle-aged substitute. Still, I knew exactly what he was suggesting.

There was a ditch at the end of the garden and when we got there Brenin began to run up and down it, over to the trees on the other side and back again: a display of excitement of the sort I had not seen – not from him anyway – in a number of years. When we'd left the house, I had envisaged a gentle stroll, an opportunity to sniff a few smells and mark a little territory. But something in his behaviour, perhaps it was a glint in his almond eye, convinced me that something strange was happening. And so we did something that even now I still cannot quite believe.

I had not been running for the best part of a year. Whenever I'd tried, Brenin, more than a decade old now, would soon start lagging behind. At first, I had tried to incorporate this into the run: running forward for a while, then jogging back to reunite with Brenin, before heading forward again to catch up with Nina and Tess. I think it had been the look of desperation on his face, the desperation that goes with understanding that your body will not do what you want it to any more – I was probably projecting, admittedly – that convinced me to stop doing this. Nina and Tess could still run all day, of course. But I could not do this to my old wolf brother and so my running with the pack had transformed into gentle walks.

That was how we began our last, entirely unexpected, run together. I had quickly put on some shorts, dug out my neglected running shoes and we'd set off through the woods, along a narrow path that brought us out to the Canal du Midi. For the first couple of miles we ran in the shadows of the giant sycamores. If this had been July, the trees would have been a blessing. But it wasn't, and they weren't. This was January; we were only a few days into the New Year. The *tramontane*, this time tasting of the snows of Lozère and Auvergne, swept down between the trees, a sycamore wind-tunnel. This was a run as cold as death. Every run has its own heartbeat, and this was the beat of a heart that was cold. The barren, leafless branches of those giant sycamore trees danced to the wind of snow and mountains. Our feet were soundless; our breath and the jingle-jingle-jingle of Brenin's chain were lost in the wind. We were not there.

I had expected Brenin to tire quickly. I had expected a quick return to the house. But he did not tire. Not a bit: he drifted, apparently without effort, over the ground beside me, almost like the Brenin of old, almost as if he was floating an inch or two above the earth; almost as if he wasn't dying. In fact, if you had to pick the dying member of the two of us, you almost certainly would not have chosen Brenin. The year in France had, let us say, not been kind to me. I'd spent it writing a little, thinking a lot, but most of all drinking copious amounts of young wine – I had become good friends with the wines of Faugères and St Chinian in particular. I had stopped running, and the wine had been slowly catching up with me. So here I was: soft, slow, staring down the barrel of forty and looking my age for the first time since looking my age had become a bad thing.

We reached the village a couple of miles away and soon after that there was a turn off from the Canal, down a little dirt track that ran along the edge of the village's vineyards. I was getting a little worried, because we were approaching the furthermost point of the run from our house. The cancer had robbed Brenin of a considerable amount of his weight. But even so, he would still have been around 120 pounds, and I really did not relish the prospect of having to carry him three miles home. But he glided on, apparently untroubled by the death that grew inside him. After about a mile, the track swung south and brought us to the eastern edge of the Grande Maïre. On one side there was the *maïre*, on the other there were fields scattered with the white horses and black bulls of the region. Many of the bulls were up to their knees in water. It did not seem to bother them too much.

The sun warmed us slightly, now we had left the trees behind. Even the *tramontane* couldn't quite take that away from a sun that had begun its slow afternoon descent into the sea, and danced fiercely on the wind-worried waters of the *maïre*. After a mile or so of tracking the lagoon, we reached the *digue*. We ran along here for half a mile or so, and then turned south again and we soon reached the beach. It was there that we rested and sat in the dying January sun, watching the waves wash gently onto the golden sands, sands littered with trunks of trees and assorted detritus from last week's storm. The sun sank slowly over the snow-peaked Canigou, nestled in the mountains that wrapped around the coast, south down to Spain.

The empty house was waiting for both of us. But, for a while at least, we sat and watched the sun.

I was thirty-nine when Brenin died. That is not, it strikes me, a particularly good year for any of us: an existential *fin de siècle* (in the bad rather than good way). That's when our myelin sheaths start breaking down. They coat the axons – the connections between brain cells. The more these sheaths break down, the worse the connectivity between neurons becomes, and the slower in both thought and deed we become. Thus begins the long road to cognitive and motor decline. The speed at which you are able to process information, and also move your body, increases with the frequency of what is known as neuronal 'action potential' (AP). This is an electrical discharge that travels along axons. Fast processing of information, and fast bodily movements, require high-frequency AP bursts. And high-frequency AP bursts depend on the integrity of the myelin sheaths coating your axons. So, as these sheaths break down, you will not only be incapable of thinking as quickly as you once could, you will be incapable of moving as quickly too. Myelin integrity starts to decline at thirty-nine.

Apparently, I will also have lost getting on for 20 per cent of my muscle mass. That is another thing that will have happened to me since I sat on the beach with Brenin that day. At least, that is the standard loss between forty and forty-nine years of age. I am not yet forty-eight, not quite – on the day of this run with Hugo along the Orb delta – but even so. And while it is a truism that different people age at different rates, once decline starts in any given area, that decline is – without some serious intervention – typically linear. In other words, a graph plotting our decline in one or another respect would follow a straight line. The gradient of the line will vary from one person to another, and for a single person it will vary from one capacity to another. But for each capacity, the line's descent is usually, bar a few minor local eccentricities, linear. This is the line of our lives.

I am sure being a mammal brings with it numerous benefits, but also one notable drawback. Many reptiles, for example, do not decline – not in the way mammals do. With all mammals, there is a gradual increased mortality with age: the older a mammal is, the more likely it is to be eaten, or to slow down too much to be able to catch food. The mortality of reptiles does not increase gradually with age – it remains pretty much constant until the reptile is very old.

As mammals get older, they lose the capacity for oocyto-genesis – they can no longer produce oocytes, female reproductive cells. There is no loss of this capacity in reptiles. They can keep producing young (more accurately, eggs containing the young-to-be) almost until they die. Some reptiles can regenerate lost limbs; no mammals can. Mammals typically have two sets of teeth, and once they have worked their way through them, they are out of luck. Reptiles enjoy continuous tooth replacement throughout life. Mammals therefore decline in a way that reptiles do not. But mammals evolved from reptiles. What evolutionary processes would have brought about this difference in response to the passage of time?

An animal that has evolved in a hazardous environment – one where there are many predators, for example – will maximize reproduction. That's the strategy best suited to cope with hazard. An animal of this sort will be what's known as r-selected, and this sort of selection will favour rapid development, small body sizes and a short lifespan. An animal living in an environment with few hazards, on the other hand, will face significant competition for resources from other members of the same species. Such an animal will be K-selected, and such selection will favour parental involvement, delayed development, larger body sizes and longer lifespans. In recent years at least, humans, elephants and whales are K-selected; mice, voles and rats are r-selected.

The expression 'in recent years', however, is a telling one – and the 'years' in question number, at most, the last sixty-five million. When the dinosaurs were still around – and this period also comprises nearly two-thirds of mammalian history – all mammals were r-selected: they were small, nocturnal animals, growing no bigger than rats and stuck stubbornly at the bottom of the food chain. So, according to one well-known story, I am declining in the way I am because of r-selection in early mammals, something that my later K-selection was not able to completely erase or overwrite.

So that clears it up: it's all the dinosaurs' fault. It is a little bit unlucky when you think about it. Without r-selection in early mammals, my life might have taken on more reptilian contours. Thrusting and burgeoning I might have remained, right up until I dropped. From this perspective, my mammalian life profile seems just a little unlucky – given that there clearly were other possibilities. If only my earliest ancestors had not been so timorous, then it might all have been different. If intelligent reptiles had co-evolved with us, descendants of the dinosaurs, then I am fairly certain I would be more than a little envious. I'm sure I'd conclude that in the great evolutionary lottery of life I had drawn a markedly shorter straw than them. 'Unlucky, mate!' a sympathetic post-dinosaur might respond. I suppose I might (in, it goes without saying, some extraordinarily loose sense of 'might') have been descended from mayflies: two hours and that's my lot. But just because I am luckier than some doesn't mean I'm not unlucky, all things considered.

Philosophers have had very little to say about decline and death, which is rather surprising given their centrality in our lives. And what they have said is often barely believable. For example, on the subject of death, many prominent philosophers have been surprisingly upbeat. Epicurus argued that death cannot harm us because while we are alive it has not happened yet – and so can't have harmed us yet – and when it happens we are no longer around to be harmed. Much more recently, Bernard Williams argued that immortality is overrated on the grounds that it would result in the eventual loss of our categorical desires – the desires that give us a reason for living – and eternal ennui would be the result.

While content with saying some rather implausible things about death, philosophers – Schopenhauer aside – have had next to nothing to say on the subject of decline. To the extent they do, their efforts are equally implausible. For example, Cephalus, the old man of ironic name who features, briefly, in Book 1 of Plato's *Republic*, maintains that being old and infirm is a good thing because you are no longer subject to the tyranny of 'youthful lusts'. But their failure to address the issue of decline reveals itself most clearly in philosophers' ruminations about what is important in life. These seem strangely off-target, almost as if decline is not an inevitable feature of life. Hedonists tell us to be happy. Happiness is what life is all about. But this is a life where I get worse and worse and then die. Should I not be at least open to the possibility that life is not really about that at all? If life is all about being happy, then this life, bequeathed me by my history, biology and the laws of the natural world, seems stunningly inapt. Taking my happiness where I can find it – maybe that is what it is about. But then what about the rest of life – the large swathes of it where I cannot find happiness? How do I live these presumably dominant segments of my life?

Then there is the mantra of the Enlightenment, enthusiastically adopted in the country to which we shall, in a few days, return: 'Be the best you can be!' Life is all about self-realization: shaping yourself according to a vision of how you would like yourself to be; striving, and becoming the best incarnation of this vision that is possible for you. But this overlooks the fact that, for the most part, this life is a process of becoming worse than I once was. As Schopenhauer put it: 'Today is bad, and day by day it will get worse – until at last the worst of all arrives.' I can be the best I can be at getting worse, I suppose. But this is nowhere near as inspiring as the original version.

Nietzsche tells us: be strong. What does not kill me makes me stronger. Maybe, but unfortunately something is, sooner or later, going to kill me. He adds: happiness is the feeling that one's power is increasing. This is deeply unfortunate, because for most of this life I will find my power diminishing. I would have thought that the question of how I should live this life must take this obvious fact as a starting point, and not blithely ignore it.

When I had just started my life as a professional philosopher, the keynote speaker at a conference I was attending, a very distinguished and well-known philosopher, was presented with an obvious objection to his clearly flawed argument. This was in the Q&A session immediately afterwards and so the audience was still there. He failed to respond adequately, instead opting for a series of rambling observations of little relevance. The man who had asked the question, a big-hearted colleague of mine, desisted from the questioning and scribbled a note that he passed to me: 'He can't do it any more.' Indeed, he couldn't. It was obvious. But this did not stop the rest of the audience from jumping on him like a murder of crows sensing a fatally weakened peer. This had a big impact on me. I know this is what life has in store for me. One day – I don't know when it will be but I know it will come – I won't be able to do it any more either and whether my inability is exhibited in public like this, or merely secreted away in the private sphere, does not really matter that much. Either way, this is, for me at least, monumentally sad. 'At least you will have escaped those tyrannical youthful lusts,' I imagine Cephalus muttering to me. Yes, well, that makes it all okay then, doesn't it. When some philosophers talk about life and what is important in it, I find I cannot help thinking of this old and distinguished philosopher who had done good work and couldn't do it any more. All I see is a series of rambling observations of dubious relevance.

It is at this point in the run and its ruminations, as Hugo and I are making our way back to the village along the *digue*, that my calf decides, in my view rather unnecessarily, to emphatically reaffirm my mammalian bloodline. Calf tears have been happening to me off and on since around 1997 – since those runs in Kinsale, when I used to charge down the hill by Charles Fort, just for the hell of it. My left calf first went on one of these descents and has been going periodically ever since. My right joined in too, after a couple of years, even though by then I had excised the downhill sprints from my running. But before today I'd had no problems for the past three years and thought I'd left this particular issue behind. I hang around on the *digue* for a while, to see if I can somehow miraculously stretch this problem away. It isn't going anywhere.

The rehab times for this injury have been getting longer and longer. I say 'rehab', but it is not as if I have actually done any, unless lounging around the house feeling sorry for myself, muttering about how unfair it all is, counts as rehab. When this problem first occurred, I was running again in two weeks. The last time it happened, it was more like six. I really should get it properly rehabbed this time – have someone dig out the scar tissue or whatever it is they do. In the meantime, I suppose I might as well try to be 'philosophical' about the whole thing. At my age – striding the highways and byways of these dangerous heart-attack years – of all the ways in which a run might end abruptly, a grade II tear of the calf is far from the worst.

R-I-C-E: Rest, Ice, Compression, Elevation. All the things I am not doing now, but should be. I limped home from the run this morning to find there was an immediate demand for my services. There will be no more running for quite some time, I suspect. But walking, limping, hobbling and shuffling – these are things I am going to have to do anyway. Serious illness, the loss of a limb: that might have bought me a day or two ... but this is all very familiar. My boys need to run. 'Come on, Daddy, we want to go to the beach.' And so I find myself limping heavily, perhaps a little theatrically I admit, along the 700 yards or so of path that leads to the sea. A few yards in front of me is Brenin, my older son. He's just turned three years old and sits proudly upon his first bike, peddling furiously and thankfully getting nowhere fast. Emma is up ahead, on a rented bicycle, and on the back of this is a seat that contains Macsen, my younger son, who was one year old last month. The flamingos, the *flamant roses*, have arrived early this year. When I first came to this part of the world, not much older than my sons are now, my jaw used to drop at what I thought of as these ridiculously exotic birds. But Brenin and Macsen are Miamians. 'They're not very bright, Daddy,' Brenin informs me. He's right; compared to the gleaming, orange Caribbean flamingos he sees in Miami, they are distinctly pallid.

The icy blast of the sea is a welcome relief, for a change. Brenin's lips will be blue within minutes, but he isn't going to be dragged out of there without a fight. We must play an important game – lifting him over the waves whilst simultaneously chanting the liturgy, 'UP-AND-OVER.' 'You didn't say it, Daddy: you've got to say it!' Then sandcastles – surrounded by a system of moats that would not have embarrassed Pierre-Paul Riquet, filled with water fetched from the Mediterranean by me, shuffling and shambling – their sole purpose to be destroyed at some subsequent time to be determined by the boys. Running from a distance, they perform graceless belly flops on the castles, hitting the sand hard, yipping like hyenas over and over again, aided and abetted by Hugo who bounds along beside them barking and frothing like a dog in the grip of *la rage*. I might have played this game once. But then I got old and didn't understand it any more. Perhaps I am beginning to understand it again.

I suspect children, and the dogs of children, understand what is important in life far better than adults. When I build the sandcastles, it is work: I do it for the enjoyment of my sons. When they destroy those castles, it is play: they do this for no other reason than to do it. As the castles die the death of a thousand belly flops, I can think of no more emphatic affirmation of the value of play over work. There is a joy that goes with this – the joy of giving yourself over wholly to the activity and not the outcome, the deed and not the goal. Perhaps I can no longer understand the game; but I can see the joy, I can feel it. I can hear it echoing out across the water towards Africa. And yet: we are not far away. I can see it. We're no more than a few metres away from the place where I once sat with a dying wolf, and watched the cold winter sun set slowly on his life.

This joy echoes out across the water but also back through the days of my life. An earlier time – Brenin had been dead two short months, and Nina, Tess and I had resumed our

runs together. It was a bright, cold spring day, and we had
journeyed up into the Cévennes, the mountains of the southern Massif Central. 'Col' is the French word for a mountain
pass. Today we were going to do a thirty-kilometre run
through the Col du Minier – 'the pass of miners'. I had
brought a small backpack, with a little food and water, and a
map. I wasn't going to push. It had been a long time since I
had run the long run. If it took all day, so be it.

The sun danced brightly on the cold blue waters of a
mountain lake. We had run only six kilometres, the map
told me, but already I was starting to feel it. When one has
been living at sea level, performance tends to start to decline
at around 3000 feet. We were at nearly 4000 feet, so altitude
may have played some role. But I suspect I was the main
problem. I was very, very out of shape, and the few 10k runs
I had put in back on the *digue* had not really kicked in yet.
Every time I returned to running after a lay-off, the pain was
worse than before. The run went on, and while my snarling
Achilles tendon had gone temporarily dormant – no doubt it
would wake up again later on – I was struggling badly. Nina
and Tess, too, were finding things far from easy. They
were also getting older, and the year's hiatus we had taken
from running had taken its toll. Nothing much was happening for me – there were no dancing thoughts that day. It was
just a slog.

I remember this run for one reason only. At around ten
kilometres or so we stopped for a sit down and a quick bite to
eat. The open mountaintop had given way to woodland a
few kilometres back and we sat in a little clearing by the
side of the trail. Nina and Tess collapsed, exhausted. Then,
after a few minutes, a little food, a little water, Tess rose to
her feet, moved away a few yards, and then charged at Nina

and performed the play bow. Nina leapt to her feet, as if she had spent the last few days resting, and they tore up and down the trail, play-growling, play-snapping at each other's shoulders and necks. And I could see the joy. I could see it there, in the exaggerated gape of Nina's jaw, and the exaggerated bounce of Tess's stride. Joy is not just an inner feeling. It can be seen, when you know how to look.

It was cold up in those mountains. The snows had not long departed those hills, and even at midday, clouds still clung stubbornly to the floors of the valleys below us. The sun did not warm that clearing in which I sat, but the joy of those two friends did. I had seen this sort of play many times before, of course. It was an almost daily occurrence. And when they played like this, I knew they were happy – as much as one can ever know anything about what is going on inside the mind of another. But today, it is different. I do not infer their joy: I see it. Some fields are made of grass, and others are made of energy. We walk through the former, and are immersed in the latter. Nina and Tess were fortunate enough to run through many fields of grass – and through Irish fields of barley and French fields of lavender. When they did, their joy would radiate out from them, reverberating across the open space – the clearing between us. Standing there with them, in a clearing in a wood in a mountain pass in France, I was immersed in a field of joy; embraced by it. This joy had permeated my runs down through all these years, although I did not know how to see it. When I run with the pack, joy warms me from the outside in.

It is here too, today, on this beach. Joy is the recognition of intrinsic value in life, the recognition of what is important for its own sake. I see the joy of my boys of summer; I hear it resonating across the blue water. But not just their joy – mine also. Formerly a feeling curled up inside of me, my joy has relocated to a place outside of me. There have been times in my life – too small in number, too fleeting in duration – when joy is like this. Joy that was a way of feeling now becomes a way of seeing. A few seconds – that is all. This transformation of inner to outer lasts a few seconds and then it is gone. But I'm coming to think they might be the most important seconds of my life. This transformation in joy is love showing herself. Love may last a lifetime, but she shows herself most completely only in moments.

Many people do not understand decline; they are unfamiliar with its anatomy and physiology. Injuries play the role of the waves of time. An injury washes over you, and you never quite come back as strong as you were before. Perhaps you won't notice this initially. Maybe you feel fine. But there's a weakness that has set up home in your muscle or joint – no amount of rehab will change that – and sooner or later its time will come again. First there's a little niggle, then another, then there are more. There are days when you are not quite a hundred per cent, but you go out running anyway. And that's fine: that's what you have to do – because these days will become more and more frequent. Before you know it, you are never quite a hundred per cent. But you keep on going, because that is what you have to do. First you are running at 95 per cent, then it's 90; and then in a heartbeat you are down to 75 per cent. Your distances are going down just as your times are going up. And you do not know how it happened. You think, if I can just stay injury-free for a while, clear up these niggles, if I can just get a good run at it, then I can get back to what I was doing before; get back to the distances and times I was doing before this run of bad luck started. But this misses the point entirely. Decline is a run of bad luck of just this sort. You will never get a good run at it again. The niggles, the aches, the weaknesses build up; and in the end you are just a tissue of niggles, aches and weaknesses woven together. No amount of rest will change this. You come back and feel good for a while, but it's so short, and before you know it you will be back to exactly where you were before the break. This is the face of decline, of erasure, of gradual disappearance. This is what it looks like. Running has many faces. One of these is the *digue*, a way of trying to hold back the storm surges of winter. Maybe it will hold for a while. But, in the end, we all return to the *maïre*.

It is common to think of life as a process of development. In growing older, we will come to understand what is important in life. With age comes wisdom, and if we are sufficiently assiduous and skilled in the use of this wisdom, perhaps even the meaning of our lives will reveal itself to us. Youth, on the other hand, is the time of immaturity: an existential prequel whose importance lies only in equipping us for the adult life to come. It is paradoxical then, as Moritz Schlick once remarked, that 'the time of preparation appears as the sweetest portion of existence, while the time of fulfilment seems the most toilsome'.

This paradox is, perhaps, a sign that we have misunderstood youth. It is a sign that what is important in life is not a destination towards which we are heading, but is scattered around a person's life, and exists most fundamentally in these moments when joy warms us from the outside in – moments of dedication to the activity and not the outcome, to the deed and not the goal. Joy is the recognition of something that is worth doing for its own sake; it is the recognition of intrinsic value as it makes itself known in a person's life. It is true that these moments of joy cluster together most noticeably in youth. Children and their dogs are much better at knowing what is important in life. They understand that the most important things in life are the things that are worth doing for their own sake. And the things not worth doing for their own sake are not worth doing at all. They know intrinsic value instinctively, effortlessly. For me, it was hard work. It has taken me half a lifetime to rediscover what I once must have known. Even now, there are times when I find it difficult to understand this joy, let alone feel it. In these times, I understand my fall from Grace, my exile from Eden.

Nevertheless, there are also times when my exile is temporarily rescinded. 'The meaning of life is youth,' Schlick once wrote. But youth, in the relevant sense, is not a matter of chronology, of one's biological age. The lines on one's face do not necessarily banish a person from the garden of youth. Youth exists wherever action has become play. Youth exists whenever there is doing for its own sake and not for the sake of anything else. Youth exists whenever there is dedication to the deed and not the goal. With this dedication comes joy, because joy is nothing more than the recognition of intrinsic value in life. This is a life where we all return to the *maïre*. And what redeems this life is the intrinsic value we find in it, if we know how to look.

7

The Borderlands of Freedom
2011

The race started around eight minutes ago, and I'm just cross-ing the starting line. I was about ten thousand back in a field of 20,000 plus – at least, that was the rumoured figure circu-lating in starting corral G – and there are still plenty of people behind me. I hope it stays that way. As they say: there's always someone slower than you – but they might not have shown up today. The shuffling walk turns to a scuffling jog, I cross the starting line and then ... I have to quickly make my way across to a strip of grass at the side of Biscayne Boulevard. It's not the calf – so far, so good with that – it's my bladder. Dehydration increases the risk of cramp, which increases the risk of a muscle tear, so I made sure I drank numerous bottles of Gatorade between my 4 a.m. train ride and the 6.15 a.m. start. So far, everything was going precisely as planned, and as a consequence I was beginning to feel quite sanguine about my prospects today. On my final pre-race visit to the Port-a-Loo, at a time when I was supposed to be in the starting corral, the queues were so deep and were moving so slowly I had to relieve myself in Bayfront Park, in full view of Metro-Dade cops who would have, at the very least, Tasered me if I had done this in any other circumstances. I am far from alone on this little patch of grass by the starting line – there're probably around a hundred or so men and women. We were all hanging around in the starting corrals for more than thirty minutes, and many people seem to have had the same problem as me.

With the necessaries taken care of, I get back in the race and begin the gentle ascent of the slip road up onto the MacArthur Causeway. I've more or less reached my planned full marathon pace by now – I would estimate it to be a dizzying five and a half miles per hour – and, so far, the calf has held together: now for the first tricky bit. The first part of the MacArthur Causeway provides the biggest gradient on the entire course. Some people decide to walk up it – which makes perfect sense: the small amount of time you save by running is more than offset by the extra energy you expend, energy that might be crucial from, say, twenty miles and beyond. I'm quite happy to run up it. My problem is different. I don't want to run down the other side. The calves have to bear more weight during a descent. That, of course, was how my long history of calf issues began. No one could compare the gentle gradient on the MacArthur Causeway with the hills of Kinsale, of course. But my most recent calf affliction announced itself when I was running down a tiny, barely discernible, slope where the road had passed over a canal. So I am taking no chances. I knew this was coming – I have studied the course video obsessively since I picked up my registration package on Friday – and I've always planned to walk down it. And that's what I do. When I get to the bottom, calf still in one piece, it feels like victory. I'm starting to believe that everything is going to be okay, at least as far as my calf is concerned. My general fitness and ability to run 26.2 miles – that's an entirely different matter.

As I see it, I have two strikes against me at this point. First, my training was severely truncated – I have about half of the recommended first-time marathoner's training under my belt, and I have been able to do nothing for the last two months. Second, I am not a good runner. I have no natural aptitude to fall back on. All I can do, therefore, is be smart, in other words ultra conservative, at least for the first half of the race. So I tuck in behind the 2.30 pace runners. This was not planned: before the race, I didn't even know there were such things as pace runners, let alone that they were kind enough to hold up signs for the entire race indicating the times they were running. What a wonderful idea – whoever first had it deserves canonization. I make myself as comfortable as I can behind the signs that read '2.30': the plan is now to stay there for the first 13.1. I lose them for a while at the other end of the MacArthur – there is another descent there, as we cross over into South Beach, and I walk that too. But after that, I speed up a little until I find them again, then just keep my nose down, drink four cups of water or Gatorade at every aid station – there is roughly one every mile from the three-mile mark on – and just generally relax and enjoy myself. As we enter South Beach, the new sun hangs low like a golden promise over the towered skyline. I am relieved, excited and happy.

I have lived in Miami for four years, but rarely ventured to South Beach, with its bars, restaurants and nightclubs – that's what happens when you have two young children and you are the sort of parent who has an unyieldingly authoritarian attitude towards their 6 p.m. bedtime. In fact, as I run up Ocean Drive at around 7 a.m. on this cold – by Miami standards, it's around 18ºC – but bright morning, it occurs to me that this is probably only the third time I've been here. Here, there are lots of smiling faces lining the streets, shouting and hooting at everyone – me included! Apparently, it's encouragement. Americans like being encouraged and the louder the better. Me – not so much. No doubt it is a British thing. What am I supposed to do? I could ignore them – but that just seems rude and ungrateful. I could flash an appreciative smile at each of these shrill supporters, perhaps proffer some small waves or even high-fives; but that just seems distracting and onerous. I have enough to contend with already. I'm tempted to speed up a little, to get through this part of the race as fast as I can – increase the cadence to escape the stridence. But I know that would bring disaster later on. And so I take the first option: rudely and ungratefully onwards I puff and thud.

Up Ocean Drive, with its empty cafes and restaurants, east along some streets I don't know. North past Lincoln Road, more streets I've never seen before. Then we meet the Venetian Causeway that takes us away from the beach and back to Downtown. The Causeway is a series of short bridges interspersed with small islands. Over to my left, I can see the towering hotels that line Biscayne Boulevard – the finishing line of both the half and full marathons. Eight miles gone, five to go until the end of the half marathon. The pace runners, bless them both, are spot on. At around 2.20 clock time, I find myself at the 12.8-mile mark. Now it's decision time. I can stop at the half marathon. I'm registered for the full, and have been since my faux-gouty episode back in September. But stopping at the half is an available option – I think they would even give me a half-marathon finisher's medal.

A brief perusal of my condition yields ambiguous results. I am tired – there's no getting around that. I'm certainly not bone-weary: there's still some gas in the tank, but I'm not sure it's enough to see me through the next 13.1 miles. But I suspect this conscious appraisal is really epiphenomenal, merely a pretence in which my conscious mind likes to engage, a game it likes to play. I always knew, deep down, that unless my calf went, or my legs were about to give way under me, I was going to go on and attempt the full. It's the knowing: I want to know what will break me. I can just imagine myself during the next week if I stop here – hating myself for my contemptible caution: all week wondering 'what if?' I would be insufferable. If I try and fail – if the second 13.1 is too much for me – then at least I'll know that I gave it everything I have, and I'll know exactly how far everything I have will take me. Sometimes it is enough to know.

The left lane turns off to the half-marathon finish and so I run down the right lane. The contrast is glaring. The half-marathon finish – that is a swarming lane of smiling faces and happy shouts, of fist pumps and raised arms, enveloped by the cheering throngs of friends and families. The marathon lane is largely empty, mostly silent: the road of the damned rather than the saved. I give Emma a quick call – my mobile phone was tucked away in my running belt for just this eventuality – and let her know not to bother coming in to meet me for another few hours. And then I run on over the 4th Street bridge to my fate.

I may not have been able to train for this marathon, specifically. But I have been doing the long run for many years. I did it at the beginning of December – twenty miles – and I did it back in France last summer, at least that run was not too far away from twenty miles. And I've been doing it, off and on, all the way back to my days in Alabama. When the pack that ran with me was young, I would run long and hard, because that is what they needed. Sometimes they would wake me up in the mornings, bouncing off the walls and I knew we were going to run twenty miles today just for fun. As they grew old, our running would taper off – maybe five stolid daily miles. And after that, just gentle walks. When they die, the pack eventually becomes young once more and the cycle begins again. These two decades of running, even if intermittent, have got to count for something today, I tell myself, and I'm sure they will. But for how much, exactly, is something I am just going to have to find out.

When you are starting to run, or working your way back after a long lay-off, your run is likely to contain multiple episodes of what I, quite recently, decided to call the 'Cartesian phase' – after the seventeenth-century French philosopher René Descartes. According to Descartes, the body, which for Descartes' purposes incorporates the brain, is a physical object, differing only in the details of its organization from other physical objects. But the mind – or soul, or spirit, or self, Descartes was comfortable thinking of these interchangeably – is very different. The mind is a non-physical thing, made up of a different substance and obeying different laws and principles of operation than physical things. The resulting view, Cartesian dualism, sees each one of us as an amalgam of two very different things: a physical body and a non-physical mind.

The Cartesian phase and I go back many years together. Today it makes its first appearance – no doubt there will be others – sometime after the fourteen-mile marker. Just get me to fifteen, I tell my legs, then you can walk for a while. But of course I must make sure I am just as much a liar today as I was in November, when I was working on getting my long run back up to twenty miles. There is nothing wrong with walking on the long run – at least as far as I am concerned, although others may disagree – as long as you absolutely have to. One way of approaching a marathon when one is in an inconveniently under-trained state is by deliberately inserting periods of walking into the race. For example, one might run for twenty minutes and then walk for five – that was one of the pieces of advice I was offered when I picked up my race packet on Friday – or, if you prefer, run for five minutes and walk for one. For some, this may be excellent advice but I do not think it will work for me. I'm far too undisciplined. Walking, for me, is simply too addictive. If I start walking now, I'm not sure I'll be able to start running again. There may come a point when I am going to have to walk. But I need to postpone that point as long as I possibly can. And so, sometime after the fourteen-mile marker, the lies begin. But who is the liar, and who is the lied to? It certainly seems as if my mind is lying to my body. It is my body that is suffering. It is my body that needs convincing. But how can my mind lie to my body if they are not two different things? It was this kind of intuition that decisively set Descartes on his course.

In some ways, I suppose I should find these dualist intuitions surprising. For much of my professional life, dualist intuitions have simply been things to ignore. Descartes' dualism is beset with empirical and logical problems as long as one's arm. Few, these days, think that mind and body are two different types of being. Generations of philosophers have made it their business to construct persuasive arguments against dualism, or failing that to invent catchy slurs –

for example, 'the ghost in the machine' – with which to disparage the view. Descartes cannot be right. I know that. And yet sometimes on the long run I can almost believe he is. Nevertheless, erroneous or not, these dualist intuitions, these Cartesian meditations if you like, are just the beginning. The illusion of spirit is merely one way that the long run can unfold.

After a while, the Cartesian phase usually gives way to my old friend, the phase of dancing thoughts. It now occurs to me that one might christen this phase after another philosopher. This is a Humean phase of the run, after the eighteenth-century Scottish philosopher David Hume. There is a famous passage in his book *A Treatise of Human Nature* where Hume remarks: 'Whenever I enter most intimately into what I call *myself* I always stumble on some particular perception or other, of heat or cold, light or shade, love or hatred, pain or pleasure. I never catch myself at any time without a perception and never can observe anything but the perception.' When Hume talks about venturing 'most intimately into what I call myself' he is talking about what we, today, refer to as introspection. When you introspect, when you turn your attention inwards, what do you find? Hume claims, and I think he is right, that you find things like thoughts, feelings, emotions and sensations. When you introspect, you encounter what it is you are thinking, what it is you are feeling and so on. Thoughts, feelings, emotions and sensations are all what are sometimes called states of mind. Hume's point then is this: you never encounter your mind or self as something separate from 'states of mind'. Or to put the same point another way: the only way you encounter your mind or self is by encountering its various states.

I used to think the Cartesian and Humean phases were separate phases of the run, each interesting in its own way, but for different reasons. I now begin to see that there is a more global pattern at work. We might think of Cartesian and Humean phases as part of a larger process: a process of dissolution of the self. I think back to how I began this run, a little over two and a half hours ago. Then I was a thoroughly embodied self. My iPod nano was turned up as far as it would go with suitably rage-filled music – things such as Saliva's 'Click Click Boom', Rage Against the Machine's 'Killing in the Name' (believe me, 'Fuck you, I won't do what you tell me' is exactly what one needs to hear from twenty miles on), Kid Rock's 'Bawitdaba' (the live version with plenty of profanity) and perhaps most testosterone-fuelled of all, the third movement of Beethoven's *Emperor Concerto*. My bodily awareness is razor sharp, keenly tuned to any disturbance in my reluctant calf – will it go, will it hold? – and, indeed, in any part of my more or less reluctant body. What does sensation in my calf mean? What is the significance of this pain in my Achilles tendon? What is the import of this this sensation in my back? At the beginning of the run, and in its early stages, I am the indivisible amalgam of mind and body in action. I am the self as imagined by Spinoza.

In the Cartesian phase, however, this heightened bodily awareness disappears. Far from being the centre of my experiential world, the body is largely dispensed with – relegated to the gullible recipient of promises unlikely to be kept. What I have now become is a mendacious spirit: a maker of promises to be broken. This is the first stage in the shrinking of the self. The embodied self has turned into a disembodied self. The body is no longer part of what I am – not the essential me – it is simply what I am using to get where I am going. Nevertheless, despite styling itself as the master, the position of the Cartesian spirit is a precarious one. The flesh may become wise to its ruses, or for some other reason simply stop obeying. The master can quickly become the slave. The Cartesian or disembodied self is, by its nature, a troubled one.

The Humean phase heralds a further retreating of the self. The Cartesian phase of the long run is characterized by the feeling that there is a non-physical self running the show – giving the body permission to do this or do that if it meets certain specified conditions. But when I enter the Humean phase, the controlling ego begins to dissolve in front of my eyes. In the Humean phase, there is no obvious mind, no obvious controller or thinker. Instead, I am mesmerized by thoughts that seem to come from nowhere, and just as quickly disappear into nowhere. No longer the duplicitous master, what remains of the self is simply the dancing of thoughts in the empty blue sky where I took my mind to be. My mind is simply the transient configurations it adopts. The self is the dance – there is no dancer over and above the dance.

Far from being made up of different, unconnected parts or facets, I now see the long run as the unfolding of a process whereby the self is progressively transformed from the Spinozist embodied form, through the Cartesian disembodied version, to the Humean self of dancing thoughts. The long run does not have to unfold in this way. Any given run may contain all or none of these phases. And even if the Humean phase is reached, it is so quickly and easily lost again. But the run can unfold in this way. And when it does, I now understand the path I am running. With each successive phase, I am journeying deeper into the beating heart of the run.

And in this heart, with each successive breath I take, the self that I am evaporates.

The absence of the fifteen-mile marker is very worrying. The first mile after turning down the road of the damned had been surprisingly easy, almost pleasant. It was, of course, a mile dominated by the adrenalin rush that goes with starting something I have no idea if I am going to be able to finish. But the adrenalin is now long gone, just like the fourteen-mile marker, and there's still no sign of fifteen. I've become very, very tired since the last marker, and the pain is beginning – an aching in the groin and upper-thigh area. I've come prepared. I take a couple of tablets of ibuprofen I had inserted in my belt, and suck down my first packet of GU – a caffeine-infused carbohydrate gel. The fact that I didn't touch any of my four packets during the first 13.1 – that I was unconsciously saving them for something – was, I now realize, rather telling. When my calf didn't go early on, I always knew I was going to attempt the 26.2, and find myself here: a long way gone, and almost as far to go. I knew also – and I must keep this firmly in the forefront of my thoughts now – that if I made it this far, this was always going to be the hard part of the run. I'm running through some rather nondescript backstreets of Coconut Grove. If I can make it as far as the downtown Grove, see the shops of Cocowalk and once again hook up with the bright blue waters of Biscayne Bay, then I'll know I am going to be okay. Probably.

In this race I have already been through Cartesian and Humean phases, several times for each in fact. That is no surprise – but what follows is entirely unexpected. Seeing Spinozist, Cartesian and Humean phases as successive stages in the dissolution of the self, I had thought that was as far as the process could go. I had assumed that the Humean phase was the culmination. I was wrong. I am now presented with a phase of the run that I have never experienced before; a phase I had no idea even existed. Initially, I was far too surprised to give it a name. But for some reason or other I seem almost preternaturally good at finding labels for things today. As the phase slowly unfolds, it occurs to me that it might appropriately be labelled the 'Sartrean phase' – after the French existentialist philosopher Jean-Paul Sartre. The Sartrean phase is, fundamentally, a further stage in the shrinking of the self.

In the Humean phase, I discern no thinker behind the thoughts. But nevertheless I am tempted to identify these thoughts with myself. I may not be the dancer – not any more – but at least I am still the dance. I am still something. This feeling is tenacious. But it ends when and where the Sartrean phase of the run begins. In the transition from Spinozist, through Cartesian to Humean phases, the self shrinks from body–mind continuum to mind, then from mind to thoughts. In the Sartrean phase, the mind shrinks further – from thoughts to nothing. Now, finding myself for the first time in the Sartrean phase, I come to see these thoughts as not part of me at all. They are transcendent objects, existing irrevocably and decisively as things outside of me. And, gradually, like a smile that slowly comes to play on the lips, I begin to understand that this has an implication of overriding importance for my ability to finish this race: these thoughts have no authority over me.

I am getting weary, there's no getting around that. I'm somewhere past the fourteen-mile marker, but my scanning of the distance in front of me still reveals no sign of the fifteen-mile mark. I'm hurting: the pain is still pretty minor, but I shall hazard a guess and say that it is going to get worse. I wouldn't say I was suffering yet, not much anyway, but I'm not too far off that point. In some ways, I want to stop, or at least walk for a while. On a certain level, I would be delighted to do either of these things. Weariness, desire: these are reasons why I might stop. But now I realize – not a sudden realization, more like a whispered rumour that slowly becomes audible – that there is no reason that can ever make me stop my plodding eleven-minute-mile, one-foot-in-front-of-the-other progress. I could add up all the reasons there are for me to stop, I could allow these reasons to congeal into a dark, persuasive mass, but still they have no power over me. All the reasons in the world to stop are still compatible with my continuing to run – with my legs continuing their stride-by-stride onward journey. There are no reasons that can make me stop. To this extent, I am free. In fact, I suspect this is the purest experience of freedom possible for a man of my age.

In his classic investigation of the nature of consciousness Sartre defended a rather remarkable claim, one that, I am beginning to suspect, few since have really understood. He wrote: 'All consciousness ... is consciousness of something. This means that there is no consciousness that is not a positing of a transcendent object, or if you prefer, that consciousness has no "content".' Consciousness has no content – there is nothing in it. Consciousness is nothing – a little pocket of nothingness that has insinuated itself into the heart of being. To the extent that I am consciousness, I am nothing at all. And because I am nothing I am free.

'All consciousness is consciousness of something.' When I think, for example, that the fifteen-mile marker can't be too far away, my thought is about the marker and its likely spatial proximity to me. If I look up and see the marker – it is an electronic board that will read '15 miles' and also tell me the clock time of the race – then my visual perception is of the marker. States of consciousness – thoughts, beliefs, memories, perceptions and so on – are always of or about things. This 'aboutness' – as philosophers refer to it, this 'intentionality' – is, Sartre thought, the essence of consciousness.

However, no object of consciousness is ever about anything – at least, not in the way conscious states are about things. The expression 'object of consciousness' means merely something of which I am aware or conscious; something I am seeing, or thinking about, or desiring, or hoping for, and so on. When I am thinking about the fifteen-mile marker, or if I see this marker, it is an object of my consciousness in Sartre's sense. The fifteen-mile marker may seem to be about something. It is about the distance travelled from the starting line, and the time taken to travel this distance. But it is about this only because we humans – especially, in this case, we human runners – interpret it that way. In itself, it is just a collection of lights on a board. We have linguistic and mathematical conventions that associate certain patterns – whether they are patterns of lights or patterns of ink on paper – with numbers and letters. It is because of us, and our interpreting abilities and conventions, that the pattern of lights on the marker means that I have run fifteen miles in two hours fifty minutes – at least that is what I hope it will say and mean when I actually get there. But in themselves, these patterns of light mean nothing at all. In other words, the fifteen-mile marker sign is about distance and time from the line and the start, but only in a derived sense – a sense that derives from our linguistic conventions.

And our linguistic conventions derive from our consciousness. However, our thoughts, beliefs, desires, hopes, fears, expectations and other states of consciousness are not like this. My thought that the fifteen-mile marker can't be too far away is not about the fifteen-mile marker and its spatial proximity to me because I, or someone else, have interpreted it to be about this. The thought is intrinsically about things. And the same is true of my other states of consciousness.

Sartre claimed that any object of consciousness is only about things in a derived sense: what it is about, if it is about anything at all, is a matter of how we interpret it. This – and here we come to the really controversial part – is true even when the object of consciousness is a mental one. Suppose I close my eyes and start picturing the fifteen-mile marker. I form a mental image of the sign or of what I think the sign will look like. I am aware of this image, so it is, as Sartre puts it, an object of my consciousness. This image certainly seems to be about the fifteen-mile marker. But, in fact, it is about the fifteen-mile marker only because I interpret the image in this way. Taken in itself, the image could mean – be about – pretty much anything. It might represent the fifteen-mile marker. Or I could be using it to represent markers in general. Or I could be using it to represent things that display numbers, things with lights, things to be looked-out-for, and so on. In principle, an image like this could mean any one of an indefinite number of things. In order to fix its meaning – in order for it to be one thing rather than another – it needs to be interpreted. And this means that, in itself, it is not about anything. Its 'aboutness' comes into the picture only with the consciousness that interprets it. All objects of consciousness, all the things of which we are aware, require interpretation if they are to mean anything. Therefore, they are not intrinsically about anything.

Consciousness is intrinsically about things. No object of consciousness – physical or mental – is intrinsically about anything. Therefore, Sartre concludes, no object of consciousness can be part of consciousness. The expression 'object of consciousness', one should remember, simply means 'something I am aware of'. Therefore, if Sartre is correct, nothing I am ever aware of can be part of my consciousness. And since I am consciousness, this means that nothing I am ever aware of can be part of me: it is an object 'for' me – something I can interpret in one or another way – but it cannot be part of what I am.

Think of Sartre as supplying a challenge: try to point to consciousness – try to point to something that is in consciousness. As you say, 'Here it is!' – mentally pointing to a thought, experience, feeling or sensation, for example – this becomes an object of your consciousness and so is, if Sartre is correct, precisely not a part of your consciousness; it is not part of you. The entire world is outside you – for the world is simply a collection of things of which you are aware; or, at least, of which you can be aware if your attention is suitably engaged. Therefore, consciousness can be nothing at all. Therefore, Sartre concludes, consciousness is simply a pure directedness towards the world – a 'wind blowing toward the world' as he once put it. Consciousness is a directedness towards things that it is not and it is nothing more than this. From this perspective, the error of Descartes was to think of consciousness as a thing – albeit a thing of a special sort, a non-physical thing, a spiritual substance. Consciousness, in reality, is no-thing. It is nothing. The error of Hume was to suppose that the thoughts, feelings and other mental states of which I am aware are parts of me. They are not: they are outside me, irreducibly alien to me.

*

All the reasons I have to stop running have no authority over me because they are not part of me. They are not part of me because I am aware of them. Because I am aware of them, they are not intrinsically about anything; their meaning is not intrinsic to them. Whatever meaning they have is something I must assign to them. And this assignation is my choice. This is the core of the argument of Sartre's monumental early – and best – work, *Being and Nothingness*. Everything else in those six hundred pages is merely an attempt to work out the implications of this idea that consciousness is empty: there is nothing in it; it has no content. I have never before understood Sartre as well as I do today, in these anxious, vicious minutes as I scan the distance for the fifteen-mile marker.

A reason is something I am aware of. If I am not aware of it, then it is not a reason, but something else – a cause. But if I am aware of a reason, then it is not a part of my consciousness. As something I am aware of, a reason can mean anything at all. In order for it to mean one thing rather than another, I must interpret it. And this means that no reason can ever compel me to do one thing rather than another. Whatever implications the reason has for my action is a matter of what that reason means. And, since the reason is something I am aware of, its meaning must come from me. Therefore there will always be a gap between reasons I have and the things I do, and there is nothing in the reasons themselves that can bridge this gap. Freedom lies in this gap. I am free to the extent that my reasons cannot compel me. And so today, somewhere past the fourteen-mile marker, I come to properly understand, for the first time, the gap between reasons and actions. The gap is always there – between every reason I have and every action I perform – but perhaps it is only on this long and difficult run that this abstruse logical point receives vivid experiential confirmation.

Every step I am going to take on the remainder of this run is a choice. Choices can be made on the basis of reasons, but I now understand that no reason can ever compel a choice. There is always a gap between the reason and the subsequent choice. At every step I take in the long run, I have a choice to make: to take another step or to stop. The only thing I cannot choose is whether or not to make this choice, and there is no reason that can compel me to choose one way or the other. At the 12.8-mile mark, I decided I was going to go on and try to run a marathon, and I have very good reasons for wanting to complete this race. But each new step requires a reaffirmation of my decision. Each new step requires a reiteration of my desire. At each new step I take in this long run, my desires and decisions can mean different things. Perhaps I shall regard them as utterly binding, or perhaps I shall see them as merely the caprices of a previous hour that should now be discarded. What they are, how they should be interpreted, that is my choice. And nothing can ever make me choose one way rather than another. An old memory briefly flashes through my mind, of Alan Sillitoe's novella, *The Loneliness of the Long Distance Runner*, whose anti-hero Colin Smith walks away a few yards from the finish line, even though he is winning and the consequences of this action will, for him, be grim. But fuelled by this Sartrean realization, I'm in far too upbeat a mood to be detained by this sort of negativity. Smith chose to stop, because there was no reason that could compel him to continue. My concerns point firmly in the other direction: there is no reason that can make me stop. No reason at all. If I stop, it will be because I have chosen to. If I stop, this will be because I have allowed a reason to deceive me – to convince me that it is more powerful than it really is.

Out of the corner of my eye I see it: the fifteen-mile marker. Hah! Not fifteen: sixteen! Apparently, I had missed the fifteen-mile marker – that's what happens when you become overly preoccupied with neo-Sartrean ruminations. Sixteen: just ten miles to go – less than two hours. I can do that. Sartre used the term 'anguish' to describe one's experience of one's own freedom. When I realize that no reason I have can ever determine what I do, then, Sartre says, I experience *angoisse*: anguish. I wouldn't call it that at all. Even before I saw the sixteen-mile marker, I wouldn't have called it that. When I understood that no reason could ever make me stop, what I experienced was joy. Joy – the most reliable symptom of what is intrinsically valuable making its presence felt in life. To run on in freedom – to run in the freedom of the gap between reasons and actions – is one of the intrinsically valuable ways of being in this world. To run in this freedom is to run in joy.

I am now beginning to suspect that Sartre's view of freedom is widely misunderstood. Some people think he is claiming less than he, in fact, is. All Sartre is doing, they say, is describing the experience of freedom – what it feels like to be free. Others think he is claiming more than he, in fact, is. They interpret Sartre as claiming that there are no limits to our freedom – that we are free in some absolute sense. No external factors or circumstances can ever shackle us or constrain what we do. That is a silly view, and I am now pretty sure Sartre did not hold it. According to Sartre we are free in this sense and to this extent: no reason can ever compel us. For us, reasons decide nothing. This is not simply a matter of feeling free: I actually am free in this sense and to this extent. But this does not, of course, mean that nothing can make me stop running. There are not only reasons there are also causes. Reasons may decide nothing; but causes certainly can.

The difference between a reason and a cause is easy to understand in principle, but sometimes difficult to pin down with any precision. The basic idea is that reasons are things we have, whereas causes are things that happen to us. I am running today because, apparently, I want to try to run a marathon – this want or desire is part of my reason. I also need to have associated pertinent beliefs. I have to believe, for example, that today is marathon day and that I am currently on the marathon course – if I didn't believe these things, then my simple desire to run the marathon would not explain why I am now running here, in this place. A standard way of thinking of reasons is as desire–belief combinations of this general sort. Together, the combination explains why I am running. Contrast this with a very different explanation. I am running because someone has tied me behind their car, and is driving the marathon course, on marathon day, at roughly five and a half miles an hour, with me in tow. This would be a cause of my running – and this cause is not something that I have; it is something that has happened to me. It is common to think of reasons as a species of cause – causes that we have rather than causes that merely happen to us. I am free, Sartre argued, to the extent that my reasons cannot compel me. But this is, of course, compatible with the idea that causes – the causes that happen to me, not the ones I have – can compel me. And obviously they can: indeed, not merely compel me, they can crush me.

There is nothing in consciousness; it is empty, a wind blowing towards the world. Consciousness is akin to a hole in being. But holes can't exist by themselves. A hole is defined by its edges, and these are not part of the hole. So a hole can exist only if there is something that is not a hole. The same is true of consciousness. Consciousness can only exist if there is something that is not consciousness. Indeed, for Sartre, consciousness is defined by its relation to things that it is not. Sartre often put this by saying – perhaps a little unhelpfully, but he was, after all, Parisian – that I am what I am not and I am not what I am. Suppose I am conscious of the things that I am, or the things I could be said to be. I am a 48-year-old man, a husband and a father of two; I am a professor of philosophy; I am from Wales, but am now a resident of Miami; I am a mediocre runner; I am severely undertrained. All these things are true of me; all these things I think I am. However, Sartre argued, I am really not any of these things. I am aware of being these things, and therefore am not any of these things. Rather, I am that which decides the significance of these things, what these things mean. Sartre argued that what I really am must escape these sorts of characterizations and any other ones that I might put in their place. What I really am always slips away from, and so cannot be captured by, the ways in which I think of myself. This is what Sartre means when he says I am not what I am. But there is also a clear sense in which if I am not a 48-year-old, running, philosophy-professing father of two who was born in Wales and is a resident of Miami, then I am not these things in a very different sense than the one in which I am not a blind blues guitarist, or the female CEO of a multinational company. I am defined as not being a 48-year-old, running, philosophy-teaching father of two, born in Wales now living in Miami. But I am not defined by my failure to be any of these other things. For Sartre, I am defined by not being what is true of me. I am not defined by not being what is false of me. This is what Sartre meant when he said that I am what I am not.

I am defined by not being what is true of me. As consciousness, I am nothing. But nothing can only exist as a relation to something. And the something that I am not is what Sartre called my 'facticity'. Facticity is equivalent to the edge of the hole – the thing that is not a hole but without which the hole cannot exist. I am not my facticity, but can exist only in relation to it. Facticity changes from moment to moment. My current facticity is, roughly, the situation in which I now, at this time, find myself. My current situation is that I am running, or at least trying to run, a marathon. I have no natural aptitude for this, quite the contrary in fact. I haven't been able to train very much; in fact training has gone very badly indeed. Then there is my specifically bodily facticity – the bodily baggage I bring to this situation. This body is forty-eight years old. It's been around the block. It has history. There are certain criminal elements of it that have what we might call 'form'. I am a tissue of injuries, scars and weaknesses sown together in the mere semblance of a man. If I hadn't been so focused on my calf issue, there would have been plenty of other things for me to worry about.

There are, for example, my arthritic knees. There's my failing back, which will occasionally go into spasm during the course of a long run (one reason I always carry a mobile phone with me these days). There is my almost constantly complaining Achilles tendon – which, I am pretty sure, is a ticking time bomb. There is my recently torn calf, and my resulting lack of anything remotely approaching marathon fitness. It is my facticity that explains why I am not going to breeze through today's 26.2 miles. Maybe I am not my facticity; but it is my facticity – rather than someone else's facticity – that therefore defines me. I am not Mark Rowlands: forty-eight, untalented, under-trained, overweight, with questionable calves, knees, Achilles and back. My facticity is a ridiculously undercooked facticity. I'd much rather I had the facticity of someone younger, lighter, or who had four months of unblemished training behind them. But that is not the way things turned out.

When you are working with this sort of facticity, then pain during the long run is entirely normal and is something I generally try to ignore rather than address. Some think of pain as a warning sign. But pain is part of my facticity. If I stopped running every time I felt a little pain, I'd never get any running done at all. Now, closing in on the nineteen-mile mark, I've been cramping up for the past two miles. My right, uninjured, calf has been the most vociferous in its complaints, and I suspect I must have been unconsciously favouring my left leg. Fantastic – rather than running a marathon, I must have been limping my way through it. Strangely, I'm not too worried about this calf, although that might simply be because I am too tired to realistically assess its condition. I tell myself that a cramp in a smaller muscle like the calf can be stretched away – and, indeed, a vigorous calf stretch every mile or so has done the trick so far. And even if it goes, I further tell myself, goes like my left one did a couple of months ago, I can limp the last seven miles to the finish line – although given that I've never limped seven miles anywhere in my life, I can hardly be certain of this.

Shortly after the nineteen-mile mark, my hamstrings start to tighten noticeably. But again I am able to effectively stretch them out. Around this time also, I am buoyed by the appearance of the five-hour pace runners. I haven't seen them since

I continued on to the full marathon. They pass me when I'm closing in on the twenty-mile mark, and I shove my tightening, hurting muscles into the little box of what does not matter, and dig in behind them. Two months ago, I would have been devastated by a time of five hours. Today, I would regard it as a result.

It's around the twenty-three-mile mark – as I am running east over the Rickenbacker Causeway – that the cramp really starts to hit hard; and this time it's in a big muscle group, my quads – both of them. This is much more difficult to stretch away. It's partly because I'm so tired, and tend to topple over every time I stand on one leg to do a quad stretch. But even when I manage to stay upright for more than a few seconds, the quad stretches just don't quite seem to be doing it. Cramp in the quads is a lot more worrying than in the calves. I may be able to limp home on shattered calves, but if a big muscle group like the quads go into spasm, I'm going to go down like a ton of bricks. And I doubt I'll be getting up any time soon. I'm three miles away from the finishing line, but I might as well be three hundred. I manage the problem as best I can: I stretch, then run as far as I can until I feel them starting to spasm, and then stretch some more.

When you run in pain, you are running on the borderlands of freedom. You still belong to the land of reasons, but are flirting dangerously with the line that marks the land of causes. The last long run I did, at the beginning of December, I began during an arthritic flare-up of one of my knees. I forget which one, but I do remember that the first eight miles or so were very unpleasant indeed; but after that it seemed to sort itself out. The pain in my quads today I judge to be considerably less than the pain in my knee then. But on that run I wasn't skirting the borderlands between reason and cause. That is the difference.

The pain in my knee was a reason to stop. But it was never going to become anything more than a reason; and no reason can ever compel me. The pain in my knee was manageable, it would get no worse and my knee would not seize up. The pain in my quads is quite different. It has everything to do with possibilities: it has little to do with what is happening now – the level of severity of the pain – and everything to do with what might happen in a moment.

Suppose I somehow knew that this pain would not lead to any more severe cramping, of the sort that would deposit me on the tarmac as if I'd been shot. It doesn't really matter how I knew this. I might imagine, for example, that there is a God kind enough to take an interest in my fortunes during this race, and He appears to me on the Rickenbacker Causeway. God tells me: okay, Mark, the pain is what it is. But it's not going to get any worse. Your quads are not going to cramp any more than they already are. You don't have to worry about collapsing in a broken heap on the ground. Just keep doing what you're doing, and you'll finish the race. If I knew this, could I keep running? Yes, without a shadow of a doubt. It wouldn't be entirely pleasant. But it would certainly be bearable.

The borderlands of freedom are the shadow lands – populated not by the concrete and reassuring what is, but by the shadows of what might come to be. When I run in this sort of pain, I run the borderlands – skirting the line that divides reasons and causes. Pain – certainly moderate pain of this sort – is a reason, and can never make me stop running. But this particular pain is a reason of a special sort: a reason that signifies the imminent appearance of a cause that can crush me.

The pain in my knee of two months ago was not this sort of pain at all, even though it was significantly more severe. It was what it was: it signified the imminent appearance of nothing. With the pain of today, I must push and push and push, right up until the last second: the second before the transformation occurs – the moment when a reason that I have becomes a cause that simply happens to me. I must push and push on to the borderline of the land of causes. But I must not step over.

8

Gods, Philosophers, Athletes
2011

That was how an ageing philosopher and talentless runner finished his first marathon: running, stretching, running, stretching, running, stretching, walking when there was no other choice, skirting the borderlands of freedom for the last three miles from the Rickenbacker Causeway to Bayfront Park. That was the deepest I had ever journeyed into the heartbeat of the run. In the gap between reasons and actions – the gap where Sartre found anguish but I found joy – I encountered one of the more surprising forms that the experience of intrinsic value can take. Maybe one day I will go deeper, if there is a deeper. My thoughts upon crossing the line: is that it? Can I stop running now? Then someone put a shiny medal around my neck, and I decided I probably could. It would have been nice if some more appropriately triumphant thought had taken the trouble to make its way into my head as I crossed the line; but I suppose that was never what it was about. 5.15:23 clock time, 5.08:44 chip time (because of the number of runners, there is a delay between the time of the gun and the time I actually cross the starting line. There is a little chip in my number bib, given to me by the race organizers, and this records the time elapsed since I crossed the starting line. This time is what is known as 'chip time'). My quad-cramping issues cost me about fifteen minutes over the closing three miles. They are pathetic times really and a couple of months ago I would have been a seething mass of malefaction. But today – facticity being what it is – I am far from unhappy.

What was the point of these last few hours, these 26 miles and 385 yards? Was it really worth it? That is the beauty of it – there was no point. It is in the places where points and purposes of life stop that you find things that are 'worth it'. We live in a utilitarian age where we tend to think of the value of everything as a function of its purpose. The defining question of our age is: 'What is it good for?' And to say that something is 'good for nothing' is equivalent to saying that it is worthless. This, as Martin Heidegger put it, is our *Gestell*, our enframing, and it is one that requires us to think in a quite specific way about what is of value in life. If something is worth doing in life it must be for the sake of something else. If running is worth doing – whether it is a marathon or a gentle jog around the block – then it must be worth doing because of the health it promotes, the sense of satisfaction or self-worth it engenders, the stress it relieves, the social opportunities it affords. If an activity is valuable at all, it must be useful for something. And the implicit assumption, one built into our defining *Gestell*, is that this something is something *else* – something outside the activity.

I see the consequences of this attitude every day, in students who tell me, 'I really wish I could have done X' –

philosophy, literature, languages – 'but my parents told me
I had to do something sensible, something useful – something that would get me a job afterwards.' And so their
young lives are already set on a course they never really
wanted. They will work to get paid, and any satisfaction
they find in life will probably have to be found elsewhere.
In another time, another *Gestell*, their parents might have
said: find something that for you is play, something you do
for its own sake, and then find someone who will pay you to
do it. But no matter how much money this is, try to make
sure you always do it for its own sake and not the money:
try to make sure it is always play, never work. I hope that is
what I shall tell my children.

There is another consequence of the way we think about
value, perhaps slightly less obvious but equally pernicious: it
makes it impossible for us to understand the value or meaning of our lives. In his essay 'The Myth of Sisyphus' the
French existentialist philosopher Albert Camus wrote:
'Killing yourself amounts to confessing. It is confessing that
life is too much for you . . . it is merely confessing that life "is
not worth the trouble".' From this perspective, which I think
is an illuminating one, the search for a meaning in life is the
search for something that makes it worth the trouble. The
idea that the value of anything in life must lie in its point or
purpose makes it impossible to find meaning in life – at least,
it makes it impossible given the way the idea of a purpose is
usually understood. To see why, consider this, characteristi-
cally dense, passage from Heidegger:

> When an entity within-the-world has already been proxi-
> mally freed for its Being, that Being is involvement . . . *with*
> this thing, for instance, which is ready-to-hand, and which

we accordingly call a 'hammer', there is an involvement in hammering; with hammering there is an involvement in making something fast; with making something fast, there is an involvement in protection against bad weather; and this protection 'is' for the sake of providing shelter for Dasein – that is to say, for the sake of a possibility of Dasein's Being ... But the totality of involvements itself goes back ultimately to a 'towards-which' in which there is no further involvement ... The primary 'towards-which' is a 'for-the-sake-of-which.' But the 'for-the-sake-of' always pertains to the Being of Dasein.

This passage is from *Being and Time*, published in 1927, the same year as Schlick's short essay 'On the Meaning of Life'. And despite some obvious differences between the two – Schlick is easy to read, Heidegger seemed to take great pleasure in being needlessly obscure – their interests overlap at this point. Suppose something can be valuable only if it has a purpose. Heidegger, in effect, shows us where all those purposes lead. '*Dasein*' is his term for human beings – or, more accurately, the type of being that is possessed by humans. Humans see the world in terms of a network of instruments, and the purposes that ultimately unite this network all point back to us – *Dasein*. One hammers to drive the nail, to make something fast, to make the house more secure, to provide protection from the storm ... to keep *Dasein* alive. Value derives from purpose, and this is where purposes end. So, if we were to take this model and employ it to try to identify the meaning of life, we would find ourselves trapped in a tautology. What is the meaning of life, what it is that makes life 'worth the trouble'? The only answer we will find is 'life'.

Nothing that has a purpose outside itself is a candidate for the thing that makes life worth the trouble – for if you follow that purpose to its logical conclusion, you will simply find more life. There is a way out of this tautological circle, the only way out, as far as I can see: to find activities where the chain of purposes ends. If we want to find value in life, something that might be a candidate for life's meaning or one of its meanings – then we must look to things that have no purpose. Put another way: it is a necessary condition of something being truly important in life that it have no purpose outside itself – that it be useless for anything else. Worthlessness – in this sense – is a necessary condition of real value. If the value of something were a matter of its utility for something else, then it would be this something else that is the locus of value.

So, as Moritz Schlick also concluded many years before I got there, if we want to find what is valuable in life we need to look to things that carry their purpose – and so their value – within themselves. And, also courtesy of Schlick, it is clear what these things are. The things we do that are valuable for their own sake are all forms of play. And running, at least for adult humans, is the oldest and simplest form of play there is. We can run for many reasons, and most of these are instrumental and so form the basis only of instrumental value. But the real value of running eclipses this instrumental value, and on its own makes running 'worth the trouble'. The purpose and value of running is intrinsic to it. The purpose and value of running is simply to run. Running is one of the places in life where the points or purposes stop. As such, running is one of the things that can make life 'worth the trouble'.

The place that gave us the marathon also gave us philosophy. That place was the city-state of Athens in the fourth and fifth centuries BCE. To understand the ancient Athenians, one needs to understand at least three things: their gods, their philosophers and their athletes. Admittedly, by this time the Athenians could no longer bring themselves to believe in their gods, just as most of us today cannot bring ourselves to believe in the God of Genesis. But they still remembered the stories and, just as it was for the stories of Creation and Fall, it is the metaphysical truth of what they remembered, rather than the literal truth, that is important.

One of Shakespeare's most memorable lines emanated from the mouth of the Duke of Gloucester, shortly after he had been blinded by Lear's daughter Regan: 'As flies to wanton boys are we to the gods. They kill us for their sport.' For the ancient Greeks, the connection between gods and their sport was indeed a close one. The reasons for this are far from accidental. In his *Letters on the Aesthetic Education of Man*, Friedrich Schiller – the eighteenth-century German philosopher, historian, poet and playwright – wrote:

> For, to declare it once and for all, man plays only when he is in the full sense of the word a man, and he is only wholly man when he is playing. This proposition, which at the moment perhaps seems paradoxical, will assume great and deep significance when we have once reached the point of applying it to the twofold seriousness of duty and of destiny; it will, I promise you, support the whole fabric of aesthetic art, and the still more difficult art of living. But it is only in science that this statement is unexpected; it has long since been alive and operative in art and in the feeling of the Greeks, its most distinguished exponents; only they transferred to Olympus what should have been realized on earth. Guided by its truth, they caused not

only the seriousness and toil which furrow the cheeks of mortals, but also the futile pleasure that smoothes the empty face, to vanish from the brows of the blessed gods and they released these perpetually happy beings from the fetters of every aim, every duty, every care, and made idleness and indifference the enviable portion of divinity; merely a more human name for the freest and most sublime state of being.

One does not have to believe in the gods of Olympus to see the significance of this passage, any more than one need believe in the God of the Old Testament to understand the significance of the book of Genesis. God or gods – they are metaphysical distractions. In each case, it is what the story shows rather than what it says that is important. There is an important truth embodied in this passage, but also an equally important error.

First, there is the truth. The Greeks 'transferred to Olympus what should have been realized on earth'. The life of a god is a representation of what an ideal human life – a life 'freest and most sublime' – would look like. The ideal life is one released from 'every aim, every duty, every care'. What would one do to fill a life such as this? To spend this life working, one would have to be a god touched by madness. Anything you might obtain through work, you can now obtain through a click of your divine fingers. The gods did not work – they played. They were immortal – what else were they going to do?

Well: I suppose sex springs to mind. An immortal creature released from every aim, duty and care – surely they would spend a lot of time having sex? It is well known that the gods were not averse to sexual encounters with each other and with mortals. But even these they tended to turn into a game. The eye of Zeus, let us suppose, has been taken by a comely mortal – Alkmene, Antiope, Danae, Dia, Elare, Europa, Eurymedousa, Kallisto, Kalyke, Kassiopeia, Lamia, Laodameia, Leda, Lysithoe, Niobe, Olympias, Pandora, Protogeneia, Pyrrha, Phthia, Semele or Thyia. Zeus had a lot of time on his hands, and his eye was frequently taken by comely mortals. There are certain advantages to being the most powerful of the gods, but also certain disadvantages. Zeus would not experience the thrill of the chase, or the agonizing of the will-she-won't-she variety. Yes, she will, if that is what he decides because he is the most powerful of the gods and she will ultimately have no choice. Consequently, Zeus turned many of his sexual encounters into games. He seduced Alkmene by disguising himself as her husband. He assumed the form of a satyr to seduce Antiope. For Europa, he took on the form of a bull – though the game here was hardly one of seduction. He assumed the form of a fellow Olympian, Artemis, in order to seduce Kallisto. The form of a swan was his preferred vehicle for the seduction of Leda. Most idiosyncratically of all, he assumed the form of an ant to impregnate Eurymedousa. She bore him a son named Myrmidon – 'ant man'. In his seductions, conquests and, it has to be said, rapes, Zeus liked to adopt an inefficient means of achieving his desired goal. He voluntarily chose to make things difficult for himself. As Bernard Suits would have put it, Zeus brought a lusory attitude to the achieving of his pre-lusory goals. Zeus liked to play, and the reason is clear: once you took away the game, all that would remain for Zeus in his sexual encounters would be a pleasant sensation in the loins. That is not to be dismissed, I suppose, but neither is it something to be making the cornerstone of one's immortal existence.

Second, there is the error contained in Schiller's claim.

Zeus is a moral monster and the same is, in general, true of his fellow Olympians. The error in Schiller's claim is to suppose that the alternative to a life of work is 'idleness and indifference'. To play is, of course, hardly to be idle. But Zeus does exhibit a notable indifference or callousness in his dealings with others. His moral failures all stem from an inability, or perhaps an unwillingness, to see intrinsic value in all the places it exists. For Zeus, intrinsic value is to be found in the game. Mortals have value to the extent they play a role in his games. Apparently, he had his moments – brief and terrifying flashes of illumination they might have been for him – when he suspected that mortals might be more than this, and at these times he would go to great lengths to protect a mortal consort. But by and large they were merely pawns – they had instrumental value only.

Today, it seems we have travelled a very different path, a mortal furrow that the gods of Olympus would find difficult even to understand. We are happy to recognize that mortal humans have intrinsic value. And we are, of course, absolutely right to do so. Some think – I am one of them – this recognition should be extended to some mortals that are not human; but the individual human being is the clearest locus of intrinsic value. The fundamental assumption underlying the ethical and political systems of the West is that all human beings are born equal: they are all equally valuable, and this value is intrinsic to them. People should not be treated as pawns in a game, merely a means to an end. People are, as Immanuel Kant – the eighteenth-century German philosopher – put it, 'ends-in-themselves'. Play, on the other hand, is typically thought of as a relatively unimportant aspect of life. Of course, one should make a little time in one's life to play: but not too much, and only when one has taken care of life's more important and pressing demands. This is not simply due to the contingencies of industrial and post-industrial life where, for most of us, it is necessary to work in order to live. The attitude runs deeper than that. Hard work is something for which a person might be legitimately praised. Play is something one merely does. To spend one's life playing – if one is fortunate enough to never have to work – is something that would draw disapprobation. We might say, of such a person, that they 'never grew up' – and that would be intended as an insult. Hard work is edifying, ennobling. Play is merely a distraction. We are, undoubtedly, morally better than the gods of Olympus. Nevertheless, at the same time, we have forgotten something that the Greeks knew, just as we came to forget what we knew when we were children. The Greeks understood that in Utopia we would play games. In Utopia, it is play that would redeem life, would make it 'worth the trouble'. But utopia is, when it is accurately portrayed, the best life a human can live. It seems we must conclude that the Greeks regarded play as an essential component of the best life a human can live. It is play, and not work, that is intrinsically valuable in life and so play, and not work, that makes life 'worth the trouble'.

Plato was the pre-eminent philosopher of the first half of fourth-century-BCE Athens and arguably the greatest philosopher ever. The safest general characterization of Western philosophy, Alfred North Whitehead once claimed, is a series of footnotes to Plato. Plato built his entire philosophical system around the existence of what he called *eidos*, or what today tend to be known as 'forms'. The form of something is its essence – what it really is. Today we talk about someone's running form – their technique. This is an echo of Plato:

the better your form, the closer you are to the perfect runner. In a slightly different sense, we might describe an athlete as being in good or poor form, or in form or out of it. Plato is very much with us today in the language we use. Even on my good days – when I am 'in form' in the second sense – I am a very long way from the form of a distance runner. Haile Gebrselassie and Kenenisa Bekele, to take two obvious examples, are both much closer to this form – indeed, of all humans, living or dead, these two might be as good approximations to the form of the distance runner as anyone. But even Gebrselassie and Bekele, Plato would claim, are not perfect. Nothing in the physical world is. What makes anyone a runner is their resemblance to or, as Plato often put it, their participation in, the form of the runner. Their status as a runner is dependent on the relation in which they stand to the form of the runner. But the form is what it is – it depends on nothing for its status. This is true more generally. Everything that exists in our world is what it is only because it bears certain relations to one or more forms. I am a man because of my (imperfect) resemblance to the form of the man. Hugo is a dog because of his resemblance to the form of the dog, and so on. But there is no converse dependence: the forms do not depend on the things that instantiate them for their existence.

The most important of the forms, and the most real, Plato argued, is the form of the good – 'The Good'. All good things – acts, rules, people, institutions and so on – count as good because they resemble or participate in The Good. The goodness of all these things is, therefore, dependent goodness. They are good to the extent they stand in the appropriate relation to something outside of them – The Good. But The Good is goodness itself, good in itself. In short, according to Plato, everything has a form. These forms belong to a non-physical realm of supra-sensible things, and in this realm they make up a pyramid of ascending reality. At the apex of this pyramid is the form of the good – the most real and most valuable thing there is.

I believe very little of this. A non-physical world of essences organized into a pyramid of ascending reality and worth: I take these claims about as seriously as I take claims about the gods of Olympus or the God of Genesis. Philosophy is a rather strange discipline where being, at least arguably, the greatest is compatible with being wrong about almost everything – and I think Plato was wrong about almost everything. Sometimes, when we discover something, an idea that we intuitively, instinctively, sense is very important indeed, we tend to lose the run of ourselves, and dress it up in metaphysical clothing that is overly extravagant and more than a little disingenuous. Religion – whether of the Olympian or Judaeo-Christian variety – is perhaps the most obvious example of this. But Plato was by no means immune to this basic human tendency. In all these cases, religious or metaphysical, what is important is not what the doctrine says, but what it shows: something important and true that is to be found crawling out diffidently from between the lines of untruth.

The Good of Plato is goodness-in-itself. Stripped of its metaphysical excesses, The Good of Plato is that which is valuable for its own sake, rather than for the sake of anything else. In other words, The Good of Plato is intrinsic value. There is no world of forms – at least I strongly suspect there is not. But there is intrinsic value. It is found in this world, not some other one; found in our lives and the things we do in those lives. In this life, it is only worth loving The Good – understood not as some otherworldly form, but as things that are intrinsically valuable. Instruments – things that are good only for the sake of something else that they might bring you – they are life's trivialities. You might want them, covet them, you might need them desperately; but you should not love them because they are not worthy of love. The love of money is the root of all evil, the Bible tells us. Or in some, more plausible, translations: the love of money is the root of all *kinds of* evil. In this, I think the Bible is absolutely correct. But this is merely a restricted version of a more general truth: love is an appropriate relation to bear to things that are intrinsically valuable. To treat things that are not intrinsically valuable as if they were intrinsically valuable – that is the root of all kinds of evil: evil lives, evil social and political systems and, often, evil people. Only intrinsically valuable things are worth loving. One of life's most important tasks is to surround oneself with things that are worth loving – and to be able to distinguish these from things that are not.

Then there is, the perhaps apocryphal, Pheidippides. According to Herodotus, Pheidippides ran from Athens to Sparta – a distance of 152 miles – to request help when the invading Persian army landed at the beach at Marathon. Other accounts, their origins and veracity unclear, claim that, following the battle, Pheidippides ran twenty-six miles from Marathon to Athens with news of the Greek victory. This, reportedly, was as much as he could take: he died immediately after uttering the words, 'We conquer!' Whether Pheidippides was a real person or not, he became associated with the origin of the race we now know, for obvious reasons, as the marathon.

For Pheidippides his run was something that presumably had only instrumental value. Some general presumably said to him: 'Pheidippides: off you go to Athens, and be quick about it. What do you mean, horse?' He was running for the

sake of something else – to spare himself whatever consequences there were for disobeying orders or occasioning a
commanding officer's displeasure. When someone starts running, or takes it up after a long absence, it might well have
everything to do with consequences. Certainly, that's how it
was with me, although I suppose the largely lupine-based
consequences were a little idiosyncratic. My life of running
as an adult, therefore, had instrumental origins.

However, no matter what instrumental reasons one has for
doing it, running has a non-instrumental essence – a form –
and this has a tendency to slowly reassert itself. At least, that
is what it did to me. When I started running with Brenin, I
was a poorly paid assistant professor of philosophy and
I could not afford a bike. Running was the cheapest solution
available to a pressing need: to dissuade Brenin from eating
all my things. However, as life proceeded and my salary crept
slowly upwards, eventually I could afford one. Indeed, a few
years later, when I had moved to Ireland, I bought a rather
nice mountain bike. But I used this only when injury pre-
vented me running with my, by then, markedly expanding
canine pack. By this point, running had me: the essence of
running – what I came to think of as the heartbeat of the
run – had established its control over me. As the pack grew
old and weakened, their destructive atrocities diminished, I
invented new instrumental reasons – little mythologies is
really what they were – to explain to myself what I was
doing. I run, I told myself, because of the clarity of thought it
induces. But I now realize the truth: I was done for. Despite
my inventions and protestations, less and less was I running
to keep a pack of canines chilled, less and less was I running
for the quality of cognition that came with it. And more and
more I was running simply to run.

Sometimes I like to imagine Pheidippides undergoing a similar transformation. The long run of Pheidippides slowly leaves its instrumental origins behind; step by step, breath by breath, Pheidippides becomes drawn into the beating heart of his run. Does he make bargains with himself? Just get me to the crossroads at Mycenae, and then you can walk for a while. Does Pheidippides become the duplicitous master, the maker of promises meant to be broken? Does Pheidippides thereby learn to spend time with his mind and so, perhaps, as Cicero would later claim, learn how to die? Does he then journey deeper into the run's beating heart? Do thoughts that come from nowhere dance for Pheidippides the way they dance for me? Does he travel deeply enough into the run's heartbeat that he eventually comes to understand that he is beyond the authority of reasons? These are the experiences of the run's beating heart. These are experiences of The Good. They are experiences of intrinsic value – one of the ways in which intrinsic value can show itself in a human life.

According to Plato, The Good belongs to, is indeed the pinnacle of, another realm of existence – the world of forms. Our access to The Good is, accordingly, an intellectual one. Only the mind, with its capacity for abstract reason, could allow us insight into the forms. It is traditional, in both philosophy and religion, to think of oneself as tied to another world, whether spiritual or metaphysical, by the mind. The mind is only partly of this world; it straddles both. But there are no other worlds. There is no heaven to which the mind goes when we die, and there is no world of forms to which the mind can travel while we are alive. Intrinsic value resides in this world, the only world there is. And our access to it is through the body as much as the mind.

This, then, is the connection between the gods, philosophers and athletes of Athens. The gods tell us that play is an essential component of the best life a human can live, something that makes life 'worth the trouble'. From the philosophers we learn that the most important thing in life is to love The Good: to love intrinsic value wherever we can find it in life. And by running in the footsteps of Pheidippides we learn that running is play and therefore intrinsically valuable – The Good showing itself in human life. Running is, it goes without saying, not the only game: the Greeks themselves invented and played many. In all of these games we find intrinsic value – what is Good in life can show itself through all of them. When running is finally taken from me, I will have to find other games to play. But running is an old game, one of the oldest and simplest there is. As such, it is one of the oldest and simplest manifestations of The Good in human activity. Running is the embodied apprehension of intrinsic value in life. This is the meaning of running. This is what running really is.

According to Schiller, the gods of Olympus would be free not only of the 'seriousness and toil which furrow the cheeks of mortals', but also of the 'futile pleasure that smoothes the empty face'. Toil and pleasure, in Schiller's view, are deeply connected. Pleasure has value in a person's life as a diversion or distraction from the toil that furrows their cheeks. So, far from being its antithesis, the value of pleasure essentially depends on toil. For example, one may decide to mark one's return home from a day of seriousness and toil by paying a visit to the drinks cabinet – 'something to take the edge off'. One may then sit down to watch a well-crafted sitcom. Both of these might be sources of pleasure. But the pleasure they induce is a function of their ability to distract or divert from the aims, duties and cares of everyday life. This is the pleasure that smoothes the empty face; it caresses only the surface of the soul and leaves no lasting impression.

There are clues to this connection between pleasure and distraction in the etymology of the closely associated word 'fun'. We do things 'for fun'. 'Fun' denotes an amusement, but also carries the connotation of a diversion. Before the early 1700s, the word was used primarily not as a noun but as a verb that meant to cheat or to hoax, and probably came from the Anglo-Saxon *fonnen*, to befool. The corresponding noun form, therefore, denoted a cheat or trick. Pleasure is a trick or hoax in the sense that its function is to distract us from just how much of life has become dominated by instrumental value. The value we place on pleasure is thus a symptom of how much our lives have become outposts of our work – of activities we do only for the sake of something else. Pleasure is most important in a life that is deficient in intrinsic value. Pleasure is the great hoax – the befooling – of the modern age.

However, also characteristic of this age is a certain way of understanding happiness. Happiness is typically thought of either as a form of pleasure or, at least as importantly, akin to pleasure. Both happiness and pleasure are conceptualized as feelings: warm, pleasant, enjoyable feelings of some sort. There may be subtle differences between happiness and pleasure: perhaps, for example, the feeling of happiness is more stable, less transient, than pleasure. Perhaps it is, in some sense that is difficult to pin down, 'deeper' or 'more meaningful'. But any difference between the two will be a difference in the type or quality of feelings. This is what is known as the 'hedonic' conception of happiness, and is contrasted with the 'eudaimonic' account of happiness favoured in earlier times. The ancient Greeks did not think of happiness as a feeling at all: for them happiness was 'well-being', living in accordance with the virtues – moral, intellectual and athletic – characteristic of humanity. Happiness, for them, was a way of being rather than a way of feeling. The hedonic conception of happiness was championed by Jeremy Bentham, the father of the moral theory known as 'utilitarianism', and has dominated our assumptions about happiness ever since. While different people have different ideas about how to produce happiness, or increase the amount of happiness in society, the idea that happiness is a pleasant feeling of some sort now goes largely unquestioned. When Richard Layard, Emeritus Professor of Economics at the LSE, and influential adviser on social policy to more than one British government, tells us that happiness is 'feeling good, enjoying life, and wanting the feeling to be maintained', and when Harvard professor Tal Ben-Shahar claims that happiness is 'the overall experience of pleasure and meaning', they are both expressing a view that is entirely orthodox.

So if pleasure is the great hoax of the modern age, and if the distinction between pleasure and happiness is a tenuous one at best, then it might seem I am committed to saying the same thing about happiness. This conclusion, however, would be premature. The problem with the hedonic conception of happiness is not that it is wrong about happiness, but that it is only half right. The hedonic view thinks of happiness as one thing – a feeling of some sort. But the concept of happiness is fundamentally ambiguous. Happiness is not one thing: it is two – and these things are very different. When understood as akin to pleasure, the same charge of trick or hoax can obviously be levelled at happiness. But this is not the only way of understanding happiness.

It is common to think of happiness as intrinsically valuable – something that we want for its own sake and not for
anything else. More than common, the claim that happiness is
intrinsically valuable is almost universally accepted, among
philosophers at least. At first glance, this may seem plausible.
We might want money because we think it will buy us happiness. But what do we think happiness will buy us? We want
happiness just because we want to be happy – for no other
reason. This is where the points or purposes stop. Therefore,
happiness must be intrinsically valuable. I suspect, however,
that if we think of happiness as pleasure, then happiness is no
such thing. Understood as pleasure, we want happiness for
the sake of something else: we want it in order to be distracted
from the domination of our lives by work – the interminable
instrumental round of doing one thing only for the sake of
something else. As pleasure, happiness presented itself as the
place where the points and purposes of life stop. But, in fact,
it turns out to be no such thing. When understood as pleasure,
happiness is the sitcom of the human soul.

Zeus – although presumably unfamiliar with the idea of a
sitcom – understood this. Zeus insisted on the game, even
though his playing resulted in the delay and, on occasion,
the absence of feelings of pleasure. We can think of happiness
as pleasure if we like but, if we do, we should also be willing
to acknowledge that happiness may not be particularly important – not the sort of thing that makes life 'worth the trouble'.
Anyone who has played a game with any conviction, and
thinks for even a second about what is involved in this, will
understand that the game is not, and never will be, about
pleasure. I can say, with confidence, that the run of 26.2 miles
I have just completed had nothing to do with pleasure. In
fact, I can safely say that it was deeply unpleasant, especially

during the second 13.1. Nor was there afterwards any compensating warm glow of satisfaction that accompanies a job well done, something that would wash away the unpleasantness. I do remember a vague, difficult-to-pin-down, post-race sense of perplexity – a kind of 'Well, what now?' sensation – but from an experiential standpoint that was about it. Nevertheless, I would not be similarly confident in the claim that, both when running and after the race was over, I was not happy. On the contrary, I suspect I was deeply, inordinately, even disgustingly, happy. If this is correct, then it seems I am forced to conclude that not all happiness is pleasure. Sometimes happiness does not even involve pleasure.

During the race, when I understood for the first time the unbridgeable gap between reasons and actions, and so understood that all the reasons in the world had no authority over me, I was tempted, a temptation I was ultimately unable to refuse, to say that I ran in joy. Schlick also distinguished pleasure from what he referred to as 'joy'. But labelling something does neither of us any good unless we can say what this label means. And if there is any distinction at all between pleasure and joy, it is one that the modern age has rendered almost invisible. When someone talks of 'enjoying' something, they often mean nothing more than they find it pleasurable – 'fun'. This is an age of feelings. It has to be so – feelings are distractions from a life dominated by work. And so, we have come to think, what can joy be other than an especially heightened feeling of pleasure – pleasure deepened and intensified? But what I have called my joy went hand in hand with a rather brutal form of experiential unpleasantness. So in what sense, and with what justification, can I call this experience 'joy'?

Joy is the other form of happiness – the variety of happiness that cannot be understood as pleasure. As pleasure, happiness is defined by the way it feels. But this is not true of happiness as joy. I said I experienced joy when I ran in the gap between reasons and actions. But Sartre described the same experience as 'anguish'. The fact that terms with such different experiential connotations can be used to refer to the same experience shows that this joy cannot be captured by the way it feels. Joy can feel like many things. Feelings can accompany joy, but they do not define it or make it what it is. The joy I encounter when I run with thoughts that come from nowhere is, in terms of the feelings that accompany it, quite different from the joy I encountered later on today's run, when I understood that all the reasons I had, or could ever have, had no authority over me. Nevertheless, these are both forms that joy can take. In its essence, joy is not a feeling or even constellation of feelings. Joy is a form of recognition.

The more our lives are dominated by the instrumental, the more we will value pleasure. The function of joy is quite different. Joy can assume many experiential forms. There is the joy of focus, the experience of being completely immersed in what one is doing. There is the joy of dedication, the experience of being dedicated to the deed and not the outcome, the activity and not the goal. There is the joy of enduring, the experience of playing the game as hard as you can play it, of giving everything you have to the game and leaving nothing in the tank, no matter the experiential toll this exacts. There is the joy of defiance, wild and fierce: no, you will not break me, not here, not today. Joy is found in the heartbeat of the run, whatever form this takes. But, ultimately, all of these come to the same thing. Joy is the experience – the recognition – of intrinsic value in life. Joy is the recognition of the things in life that possess value in themselves – the things that are valuable for their own sake:

the things in life that are worthy of love. Pleasure distracts us from what does not have intrinsic value. Joy is the recognition of what does. Pleasure is a way of feeling. But joy is a way of seeing. Joy is something that pleasure is not and can never be. It is the recognition of the places in life where all the points and purposes stop.

Most of us will leave this life in the same way we entered it: scared, confused and alone. But when we came into this world we were met with loving arms and soothing words. On the way out of it, we will be met by nothing. The life of every living thing follows these general contours, and to this extent life is sad and deeply unfortunate. But with humans, it is something else. I used to worry about what the future had in store for me, and this, I suppose, is bad enough. But I know that this is what life has in store for my children also, and that is far worse. Sometimes, as Wittgenstein once remarked, the most difficult things to see in life are the most obvious, and they are the most difficult to see precisely because they are the most obvious. This now seems obvious to me. I can do nothing of any great significance to protect my children from life and this evil place to which I have brought them. To be sure, I can help out a little when their lives are going well, when they are growing, burgeoning and their encounters with intrinsic value in their lives crowd most thickly. But when the going gets tough, I'll be out of here like the worst deadbeat dad. In a few short decades – and that is assuming I have a few decades left in me – I shall abandon them to face their gradual disappearance without me. But can I live on in their memories, and provide for them a powerful example of how to live in this malignant place and how to face their gradual disappearance? Perhaps, but unfortunately the memories we make when we are young are sickly children. My sons have no need of memories yet – why would they? And by the time they do, I shall no longer be around to be remembered. As Milan Kundera once remarked, before being forgotten we are transformed into kitsch. The memories that remain of me will be caricatures, vague suggestions or themes where a man used to be. For we humans, understanding our fate is part of our fate. And because of this the fate of those we love becomes part of our fate. This means that our lives are more than sad or unfortunate: they are tragic. Tragedy is born when misfortune and understanding meet: when one not only suffers and dies but at the same time understands that this suffering and death is irrevocable.

If there were a meaning to this life it would be that which redeems it. It would be something that, as Camus said, makes life 'worth the trouble'. Nietzsche went further than this – a meaning in life must allow us not merely to endure life, but to love it: 'My formula for greatness in a human being is *amor fati*: that one wants nothing to be different, not forward, not backward, not in all eternity. Not merely bear what is necessary, still less conceal it – all idealism is mendacity in the face of what is necessary – but love it.' *Amor fati* – the love of fate – is a lot to ask. Sometimes I can almost deal with backward. I've been very fortunate in my life. But even so, it is truly difficult not to regret at least a few of my past idiocies or indiscretions. Some people tell me they would not change a thing. Personally, I suspect I would. But backwards pales into insignificance when you compare it with forwards. To love this fate is, I suspect, an impossible task.

And yet, there are moments when I come close. Fundamentally, there is a difference between a life that is lived chasing what is important and a life lived immersed in and surrounded by it. The two types of life are separated by a vast, unbridgeable chasm. There are those who run in order to chase something else. And there are those who run simply to run. To the extent there is a meaning to be found in this life, I cannot see how it could be anything other than this: do not chase, just run. A life dominated by instrumental value is a life spent chasing, of hunting down one thing for the sake of something else. Instead, find what is Good in life, love what is Good in life, surround yourself with it and hold on to it with all the strength you have.

Running and the pack, both canine and human: these have consistently been the twin poles of intrinsic value – The Good – in my life. When I run, I am immersed in The Good. When I run with my pack, although the pack will change, I am surrounded by The Good. We cannot always find a pack – circumstances sometimes conspire against us in that way. But it is still possible to find The Good. To do that, it is enough to put on a pair of running shoes and keep running until you find yourself in the run's beating heart. If you keep going, it will happen in the end.

In these moments when I am immersed in and surrounded by The Good, if I cannot love fate I am at least reconciled with it. I am reconciled with fate because I am unable to make myself care enough to wish that it were different. This is hardly the same as loving fate – but it is an accommodation. And that is the best I can do. For these brief moments, nothing that has happened before, nothing that will happen after is of the slightest consequence. I would no more desire a difference in the past or future than I would request that a lizard that bathes in the sun, as the pack and I drift past, be moved from one basking rock to another. In these moments, my fate has no dominion. I cannot love my fate, but I can at least be as impassive as it is, as impassive as the rock on which the lizard lies. In these moments, at least, I am equal to my fate. In these times when all the points and purposes of life stop, that is where the chase ends and the run really begins.

In the beating heart of the run, I hear an echo of what I once was and what I once knew. When the heartbeat of the run embraces me, holds me tight, I am returned to what I was before the fall. When the rhythm of the run holds me tight, I run in a field of joy. Surrounded by it, warmed by it from the outside in. In these moments, the run whispers to me: her whispers are the thoughts that come and go, out of the blue and into the black. She whispers to me a truth that I once knew but could not remember, like a dream that stood and slowly faded just beyond the edges of recall. These are whispers of joy, of what it is to be free, and of what is truly important in a life like this – a life that holds us naked and dying. She whispers to me of my time in Eden.

Acknowledgements

My thanks to my editor, Sara Holloway, for her patient and invaluable advice over the months as this book slowly took on its final form, and for encouraging me to follow the emerging thoughts wherever they led. Thanks to Anne Meadows who was kind enough to read an entire draft of this book and made some very useful suggestions. Thanks also to Benjamin Buchan for his excellent copy-editing, and to Miranda Baker for excellent proofreading and more.

Thanks, as always, to my agent, Liz Puttick. My thanks also to the magic fingers of Bruce Wilk, the physiotherapist who succeeded in breaking down decades of scar tissue in my left calf – efforts without which the events that formed the basis of Chapters 1 and 7 would never have happened. No doubt, I shall be seeing you about my right calf in the not too distant future.

I'm almost convinced that running is a place where I channel long-forgotten thoughts: of thinkers read and largely forgotten, of thinkers buried long ago and whose thoughts have similarly been buried somewhere in my brain while it goes about its day-to-day business of keeping me alive and mostly sane. Many of the thoughts which brushed by me when I ran, almost like I was standing still, and which find their way into this book in various ways, are the thoughts of people such as Plato, Moritz Schlick, Arthur Schopenhauer, Jean-Paul Sartre, Friedrich Nietzsche, Martin Heidegger, Aristotle, David Hume and René Descartes.

Most of all, my greatest debt is to the pack that has been good enough to share its life with me, and helped me understand the difference between a life spent chasing what is important and a life spent immersed in it. Thanks, first, to my canine pack. Thank you Boots, Pharaoh, Sandy, Brenin, Nina, Tess and Hugo, for sharing the trails with me over the years: lazy so-and-so that I am, I probably would never have run them without you. Thanks to my human pack. Thanks to my mother and father, for ensuring my life was never going to turn out dogless. Thanks to my sons, Brenin and Macsen, for reminding me, each in your inimitable way, of something I had long forgotten – something, indeed, that I was destined to forget. And, finally, thanks to Emma, whom I believe I once described as the most beautiful woman I've ever met and the kindest woman I've ever known. I wasn't wrong.

Index

Index

exhaustion, 51–2

facticity, 44, 175–6, 181
faith, 8–9
feelings, 199–200
flamingos, 147
flatfish, 72–3
forms, 189–91, 194
freedom, 21–3, 172–3, 178, 204
   of age, 24, 44
   and knowledge, 29–31
   of youth, 20–1, 23–4, 44
frontal cortex, 50, 54
fun, 196

games, 89–94, 96, 187–9, 195, 198, 200
gamma oscillations, 50–1, 53–4
Garonne, river, 136
Gebrselassie, Haile, 40, 190
genes, 124, 126–8, 130
genetic fallacy, 126
Gestell, xii, 181–2
gluteus maximus, 66
Good, The, 190–1, 194–5, 203–4
gorillas, 66
gout, 10–13
grasp over reach hypothesis, 18

happiness, 144–5, 196–200
Hardrock, 16–17
hedonists, 144
Heidegger, Martin, xi–xii, 181–3
Heinrich, Bernd, x, 7, 42